Demystifying
TCP/IP

Ed Taylor

Wordware Publishing, Inc.

Library of Congress Cataloging-in-Publication Data

Taylor, Ed, 1958-
    Demystifying TCP/IP / by Ed Taylor.
      p. cm.
    Includes index.
    ISBN 1-55622-400-1
    1. TCP/IP (Computer network protocol).   I. Title.
    TK5105.55.T387   1993
    004.6'2--dc20   93-32049
                                                  CIP

ISBN 1-55622-400-1

10 9 8 7 6 5 4 3 2

9308

All inquiries for volume purchases of this book should be addressed to
Wordware Publishing, Inc., at the above address. Telephone inquiries may be
made by calling:

(214) 423-0090

Contents

Acknowledgements

Ted
Zac & Lulie
Dell Computer Corporation
George Wynn
O. E. Perry
Jerry Perry
Kyoko Fuki in Pebble Beach
Dr. Umar at Bell Laboratories
Ellen Hancock at IBM UK
Dan Lynch at Interop
Jim Woodward at Dell Computer
Ceil (from the English student)
Denny Yost
Ginny & Maegan
Don Davis (Are you working yet?)

Bob Thomas (Remember Article 1?)
Louise Herdon Wells
Johnny & Erin & Summer
Zelma (Read any dumps lately?)
Cythia Fetty
Dr. Samuel L. Gladney & staff
Raleigh Curter
Cleve, Stan, Nancy, B. J.
Bill K., Tom B., Herb C., Andrew C.
BC
Lone Star Cleaners
Corbin
Mark Lane

Dedication

This book is
Dedicated to
Nissa and Little Issac

Preface

The purpose of this book is to orient the reader to TCP/IP. Its design intent is to help those new to this topic get a jump start before moving on to more detailed books.

Chapter 1 provides background information concerning why networks and protocols are needed. What a protocol does is explained along with the concept of data flow through a network. A brief discussion explains the basis on which networks are built. The concept of a backbone is explained (from a nonhuman perspective).

Chapter 2 is the jumping off point for TCP/IP. This chapter covers what TCP/IP is, how it looks, what a client and server are, and how it is possible that TCP/IP can work with different operating systems. A look at differences between various vendor TCP/IP protocols is included.

Chapter 3 is a more detailed overview of TCP/IP. Its history and components are explained. The Internet and the internet are examined. A quick glimpse at ETHERNET is included.

Chapter 4 answers the question, "What is a TELNET?" How TELNET is used is explained along with TELNET characteristics. Explanation is provided about the concept of a raw TELNET and a TN3270 client application. Hints for using TELNET client is included and some TELNET client commands.

Chapter 5 explains what FTP is. Basic functions FTP can perform are presented. FTP commands found in many TCP/IP protocol suites are described, and a section on how to use them is included. As the section explains, there is no mystery behind FTP.

Chapter 6 presents SMTP. Electronic mail is briefly discussed. SMTP components are shown and SMTP commands are included.

Chapter 7 discusses TCP/IP addressing. Addressing is first examined in relation to the network layer involved. Ports, sockets, and IP address classification are explained. DIX ETHERNET and 802.3 are compared and contrasted. A look into how ETHERNET and 802.3 emerged is also included.

Chapter 8 demystifies X! Understanding X in relation to other components in TCP/IP is shown and the origins of X are explained. X components are shown and explained. The function of X and common terms used along with it are included. A look at how X works is presented. The X environment is also given attention.

Acronyms   This list includes many acronyms used with TCP/IP and related conversations.

Glossary   The glossary takes many obscure terms and explains them in understandable words.

Well-Known-Port Numbers   A list of these ports is provided and as the reader uses TCP/IP more, they will be more useful.

RFC Listing   The RFC listing is included for two reasons: First, if one takes time to glance through it, one can realize the evolution of TCP/IP over the years. Second, it is a helpful beginning point for further reference.

Chapter 1

Understand This First!

This chapter provides background information necessary before exploring Transmission Control Protocol/Internet Protocol (TCP/IP). Questions such as: Why Do I Need a Network?, Why Do I Need a Protocol?, What Does a Protocol Do?, Which Protocol Do I Need?, How are Networks Built?, and What is a Backbone? are presented in this chapter.

1.1 Why Do I Need A Network?

Excellent question. If you ask ten people this question, you will probably get ten different answers. Some consensus exists, however. Ask this question to financial people or managers in corporations and they may respond by saying it will help them maximize technical resources within their company. Networking can do this if properly implemented. Ask a documentation or training department the same question and the response may be entirely different. A typical response from such a department might be something like, "It would enable all workers in the departments to exchange files, have electronic mail, and have remote logon access to hosts not located on their desks."

There are reasons for having a network. Commonalities exist among most networks, but differences also exist. Three common functions in any given network are the following:

- Remote Logon. This service permits a user on his/her host to log on "remotely" to a host in a different location.

- File Transfer. This service permits network users to exchange files. It saves time and can eliminate duplication of resources. And, most of all, it is convenient for users.
- Electronic Mail. This service allows all users on the network to exchange mail electronically. The idea and function is similar to the current mail system except it is paperless, cost effective, and efficient.

Networks can (and usually do) provide services and features beyond these mentioned previously. The needs of the user and the type network implemented determine what is available. A particular advantage networks offer is that some networks support different vendor equipment, thus providing interoperability between unlike equipment. This alone is reason enough to install a network wherein lies heterogeneous equipment.

1.2 Why Do I Need a Protocol?

To connect computers, printers, disk drives, terminal servers, communication servers, and other devices requires some form of a network. For a network to function, rules and regulations must be followed. In the technical community, these rules and regulations are called protocols. Transmission Control Protocol/Internet Protocol (TCP/IP) is a network protocol that has rules and regulations which permit different vendor equipment to interoperate. This is a powerful statement. Examples will be provided later, but for now it means if a network is based upon TCP/IP, a DEC computer can communicate with an IBM, Convex, Apple, SUN, Unisys, or just about any vendor's equipment.

In network terminology, these rules and regulations are referred to as network protocols. Network protocols define various aspects of user operations. For example, a network protocol defines how a user performs a remote logon, file transfer, or electronic mail.

1.3 What Does a Network Protocol Do?

A network protocol defines all operations within a network. Protocols even define how entities outside the network must interact with the network. For example, some network protocols define how data gets from point A to point B. Other network protocols define how a computer or device communicates over a particular medium, like a telephone line or other type connection. Simply put, protocols define how things are to be done if a device is going to operate in a network.

1.4   Which Network Protocol Do I Need?

To do this a point of reference is needed. A good reference point is a model of what constituent parts should exist in networks. A standards making body called the International Standard Organization has what they call the Open Systems Interconnection (OSI) model.

This OSI model defines that which should exist in any network. The OSI model used here will be a reference point to explain basic aspects about network protocols. The OSI model consists of seven (7) layers. To better understand this, picture a cake with seven (7) layers and envision the cake cut in half; the seven layers would be identifiable. The OSI model is similar to the seven-layered cake cut in half. OSI network layers have names and perform specific functions. This model, including the layers and their names, is identified in figure 1.1.

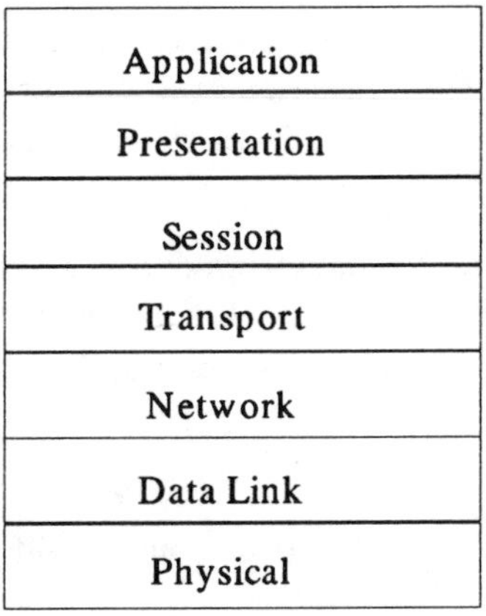

| Application |
| Presentation |
| Session |
| Transport |
| Network |
| Data Link |
| Physical |

Figure 1.1

Before we examine what each layer does, consider this. Envision a network consisting of computers, software, cables, and everything that goes into making a network. Most networks can be divided into layers.

Network layers can be explained in accordance with their function. Usually, there is not a one-to-one correspondence when attempting to explain different networks by layers. Many network protocols do not appear like the OSI model.

A layer synopsis from top to bottom includes:

Application This layer provides services software applications require. For example, it provides services necessary for a file transfer program to operate. It is called the application layer because it works with or is a provider of services to applications (in certain network protocols).

Presentation This layer determines data syntax. In short, whether data is ASCII or EBCDIC is determined here. This layer performs encoding values that represent data types being transferred.

Session This layer is considered the user's interface into the network; however, the user is not aware of it. This layer is where logical connections are made with applications. The session layer has addressable end points that relate to programs or a user.

Transport On the sending node in a network the transport layer takes data from the session layer and puts a header and trailer around the data itself. Some transport protocols ensure the data arrives correctly at the destination; this type protocol is connection oriented. Conversely, connectionless oriented protocols do not ensure this. On the receiving node the transport layer removes the header and trailer and passes the data to the session layer.

Network This layer routes data from one location to another (source to destination). The network protocol in use determines how this layer works. In the case of TCP/IP this is Internet Protocol (IP).

Data Link The main goal of the data link layer is to provide reliable data transfer across a physical link. This layer puts data into frames, transmits these frames sequentially, and ensures they have been received in order by the target host.

Physical This layer is an interface between the medium and the device. This layer transmits bits (ones and zeros). Specifically, it transmits voltage or light pulses.

Different network protocols can be evaluated with the OSI model serving as a baseline. OSI itself is a network protocol, but the focus here is TCP/IP. The OSI model will be used later in the book to explore further aspects of TCP/IP.

1.5 Data Flow Through a Network

In a network data flows from the sending node from top to bottom (with respect to layers in the network). This means that as data passes down the network protocol stack, headers and trailers are added to the data, at each layer. Likewise in a network the receiving node's data flows from bottom to top (with respect to the network layers). These headers and trailers are removed by layer as the data moves up the protocol stack.

In some cases the sending node is a terminal user and the receiving entity is an application program. In other cases both sending and receiving entities can be application programs.

These headers and trailers wrapped around the data include information particular to the needs of a specific layer. For example, the network layer header includes routing information. Consider figure 1.2 depicting the OSI model and how headers are added to data as it passes down the OSI protocol stack.

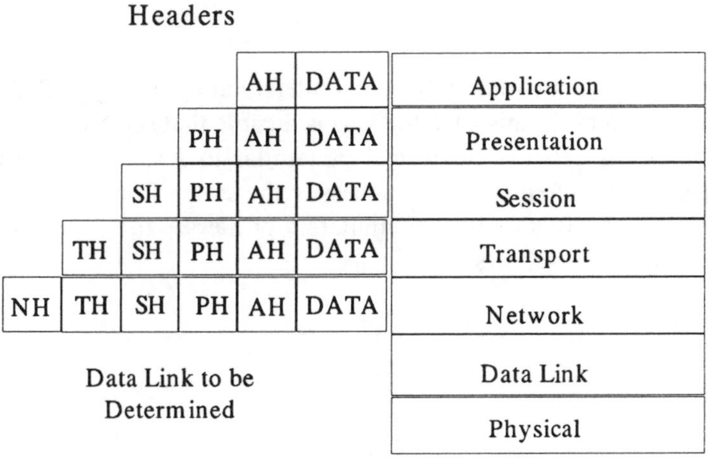

Headers

					AH	DATA	Application
				PH	AH	DATA	Presentation
			SH	PH	AH	DATA	Session
		TH	SH	PH	AH	DATA	Transport
	NH	TH	SH	PH	AH	DATA	Network
	Data Link to be Determined						Data Link
							Physical

Figure 1.2

1.6   How Are Networks Built?

It is important to know how networks are built because this provides a framework for discussions about a network. One way to explain how networks are built is to explore how network devices are physically connected to a common medium. The idea of a common medium is fundamental to many networks. Granted this common medium may span great distances and be comprised of "different" types of media; collectively the medium can be considered as a whole. Networks can consist of devices such as computers, printers, servers, etc. connected together. These devices connect to the medium directly or indirectly. The medium may consist of different types, but the common thread is these devices connect to the medium, thus a network. They may be spread out physically around the world. In the technical community, the physical layout of a network has a technical term associated with it called a *topology*. A number of topologies exist, but our focus here will include:

- Bus
- Ring
- Hub

In addition to the topologies mentioned above, two terms frequently used in discussions about networks need to be understood. They are presented after explanation of the Bus topology.

The Bus

A Bus based network can best be understood by analogy. Think of a Bus as a street. In this case the Bus is a cable that serves as an access point for all network devices. It is similar to a street because each house on any given street has access to the street. Consider figure 1.3 depicting a Bus with computers, printers, file servers, and communication servers.

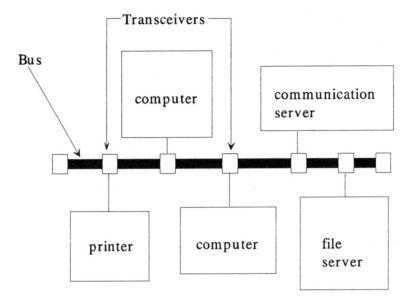

Figure 1.3

Figure 1.3 shows a straight line as the common link between all participating network devices. Notice figure 1.3 displays the Bus as a straight line. In reality this is generally not the case. Because the Bus is a cable, it usually gets shaped to fit the physical environment where it is installed.

One example of a Bus topology is where network devices attach to the cable via a transceiver. The transceiver serves as a connection point for network devices. Transceivers do more than serve as a connection point, but this is not the focus here. These transceivers have a cable that connects them to the network device interface card. This cable is typically called a drop cable. Review figure 1.3.

A Bus could be considered a data highway. It is the medium where data is passed from source to destination. Devices attached to the Bus can access it and send or receive data. In a very real sense it is a data highway.

The two terms needing understanding in light of topologies are logical and physical. Figure 1.3 shows a logical example of a hypothetical Bus network. It is considered a "logical" example because in real life the majority of Bus networks are not straight lines. If figure 1.3 were a real implementation, the line depicting the Bus would likely be very crooked.

Think about it. If a Bus is the main cable network devices connect to, it stands to reason the cable itself is probably between walls, in the ceiling, possibly under floors, and twisted about in other ways. The last thing it will be is straight.

The term "physical" is generally used to reflect the actual implementation (how it may appear). The next topology is a good example of how the terms "logical" and "physical" are used. Of course using these terms to explain a topology is a generalization, and it would be incorrect to extrapolate conclusions beyond that which is stated.

The terms "logical" and "physical" are used far beyond the bounds of network topologies. They are used in a variety of explanations, however our focus here is upon topologies.

The Ring

When a Ring topology is mentioned, token ring may come to mind. Token ring is a protocol (way of passing data) at lower layers within a network, specifically the data link layer. Most pictures show a token ring network like figure 1.4.

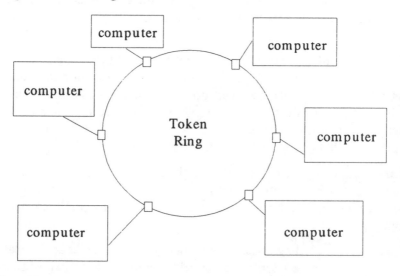

Figure 1.4

Figure 1.4 is a "logical" example of a network based on a ring topology. It *does not* depict how a token ring network appears physically. A token ring network is built around a device called a Media (some call it a Medium) Access Unit (MAU).

If one goes looking for a token ring network, figure 1.5 is an example of what will be found.

Media Access Unit

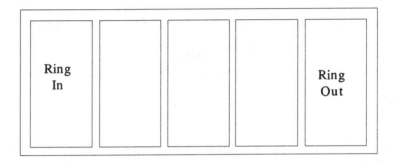

Figure 1.5

The MAU has a ring inside, hence it is considered a ring based network. Unfortunately, many diagrams and explanations depicting a ring network either assume this knowledge on behalf of the reader, or for whatever reason it is omitted.

This could be funny. Can you imagine someone new to token ring networks and asked to isolate a problem with a token ring network. If nobody told the individual there is no visible "ring" to be found (outside of disassembling the MAU) they could look for days! Believe it or not, I have witnessed this.

Other types of ring based networks exist, however they are based on the same fundamental premise. They have a ring (or two) used to pass data. The ring topology uses a cable in a ring fashion and serves as the data highway for data to get from source to destination.

The Hub

A hub is like its name connotes. It is a central point of connection. Figure 1.6 shows how a hub topology appears.

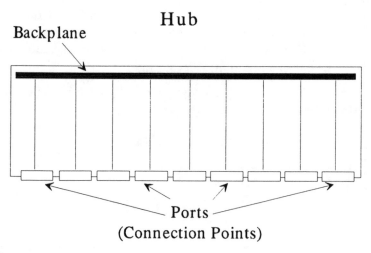

Figure 1.6

A hub is the central point of the network from a physical connection. In many cases certain type networks that employ a hub topology are easily implemented and maintained. Hub popularity has increased over the past few years, and as a result certain hubs are becoming inexpensive.

1.7   What Is a Backbone?

The term backbone is used frequently in conversations about networking. It means different things depending upon the context and point trying to be made. For example, the term backbone could be used in light of the topology of a network. If such were the case, the meaning conveyed is the physical connections and primarily the common point of connection for devices attached to the network.

The term backbone is also used to refer to a network protocol. When this is the case, a larger concept is usually conveyed. An example of this could be someone using the term to refer to routing from network A to network B *through* an unlike network, say network C. An example of this is figure 1.7.

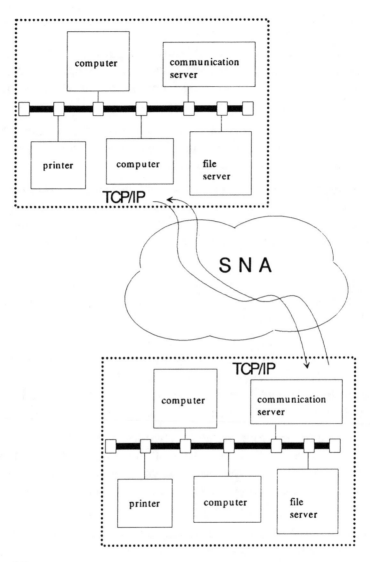

Figure 1.7

The term backbone can be most confusing, especially if the speaker or writer does not communicate precisely the intended meaning. The term backbone is not a descriptive technical term!

1.8 Conclusion

Networks can be a valued addition to a corporation or even a small company. The type of network chosen will dictate features and functions available for users, programmers, and others accessing the network.

Networks are comprised of protocols. Network protocols themselves are rules defining how things will be done such as remote logons, file transfers, and electronic mail for example.

The protocol chosen for a network should be based upon the one that best meets users' needs. Consideration for interoperability among different vendor equipment should be taken into consideration also. Other issues may need evaluation, and each site should be able to define their own needs.

The physical layout of a network can vary. The site can dictate this to some degree. But, many protocols dictate which physical arrangement must be used with network implementations.

The difference between the physical layout of a network and the logical implementation can be confusing, but it is nevertheless important. The term backbone should be understood in light of how vendors use it to explain their equipment. A variety of meanings are currently associated with the term, and as a result confusion abounds.

Getting acclimated to computer networks is half the battle. The remainder of the battle is the constant challenge to remain current, understanding the technology used and changes to existing equipment. The pace of change in network technology now is greater than when I began (or I suppose I could be slowing down).

Now more than ever companies are harnessing the power in networks to leverage company resources. On a recent trip I realized the 1980s witnessed an unprecedented expansion in technology and development of products. And as surely as this was the case, so the 1990s will be the decade of learning and dissemination of knowledge about this technology.

Chapter 2

Beginning with TCP/IP

This won't be as tough or as boring as you think, neither will it be a history lesson! This chapter presents some information that is best understood in the early phases of learning TCP/IP. TCP/IP is the acronym for Transmission Control Protocol/Internet Protocol. It is software. It is a network protocol. Remember from chapter one that a protocol of any kind is an agreement upon how to do *something*.

A network can be built using TCP/IP as the network protocol. But, in order for nodes (devices such as computers, etc.) to operate they must all use the same protocol. Simply put, they must agree upon how they are going to communicate. Since nodes cannot think as humans, the concept of configuration enters our topic of networking. Each node connected together, using TCP/IP, must be configured appropriately for it to function.

The remainder of this chapter will examine and explain the following:

- What is TCP/IP?
- What is client/server?
- How can TCP/IP work with different operating systems?
- Are all TCP/IP protocol stacks alike?

2.1   What Is TCP/IP?

TCP/IP is a software protocol as mentioned previously. It is a component to build networks. Other components are needed, but a software protocol is fundamental to any network.

TCP/IP is a collection of programs and defined ways of doing things like:

- Remote logons
- File transfers
- Electronic mail
- Providing support for custom written programs
- Providing a mechanism for data transport throughout a network
- Routing data throughout a network
- Support for a distributed windowing system

Figure 2.1 shows an abbreviated TCP/IP protocol suite divided into three sections and how they correlate to the OSI model.

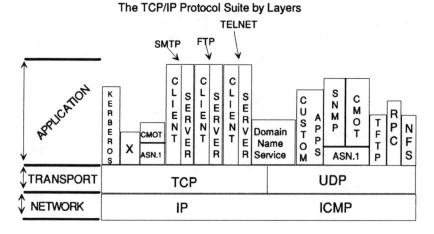

Figure 2.1

Notice TCP/IP protocols start at layer three, which as defined by the OSI model is the network layer. Based on this diagram, TCP/IP is clearly not a seven-layer network protocol. It begins at the network layer and functions there and above.

Remote Logons

If you are new to networking and TCP/IP, then the concept of a remote logon could be new also. It is as the name implies. It is an application providing a function whereby a user can be on system "A" and log on to system "B," wherever "B" might be located. The user has the perception that they are physically logged into system "B." Actually, the appearance is a reflection of a logical connection established between system "A" and "B."

This TCP/IP application is called TELNET. Normally, it is written in all caps, but other variations exist.

File Transfers

TCP/IP supports file transfers from one system to another. This is similar to the remote logon capacity, but it differs because of what can be done. A file transfer must support a remote logon to the target machine by default, but it does not provide the simulation for the user to perform interactive work on the target system in the sense that TELNET does. There is an exception.

A specific program part of TCP/IP is the File Transfer Program (FTP). It provides a user on system "A" the ability to log on to system "B" and issue basic commands native to system "B." For example, it would allow the user to issue commands to change a directory, delete a file, and perform other functions supported by the native operating system in system "B." An aspect of FTP is interesting.

FTP seems to imply a file is *transferred* from one system to another. This is not the case. What FTP does is permit copying a file from say, system "B" to system "A." The original file being copied still exists after the "file transfer" is performed.

Electronic Mail

TCP/IP supports electronic mail via Simple Mail Transfer Protocol (SMTP). From an operational standpoint, it is similar to the remote logon and file transfer support in that a client and server are involved (clients and servers are explained in the coming section).

The electronic mail program enables users to exchange messages with one another. It also provides a way whereby a mass mailing can be performed.

Custom Written Applications

TCP/IP provides support for those who need to do a special thing that is not native to TCP/IP. For example, say a need exists to transfer data from one machine to another automatically without human intervention. It can be done, and there is support within TCP/IP for this. This support is via UDP.

Transport Mechanisms

As figure 2.1 shows TCP/IP has two transport mechanisms. They are TCP and UDP. TCP is the acronym for Transmission Control Protocol, and UDP is the acronym for User Datagram Protocol. Detailed reasons as to why this is the case are presented later, but this does provide a way TCP/IP can be customized as need be by programmers or administrators.

Routing Mechanism

TCP/IP has within it a program that performs routing of data throughout a TCP/IP network. More will be explained about it later, but it is that component which aids in setting up a logical connection with a target host in the network. This component is called Internet Protocol (IP). Other routing protocols also exist.

A Distributed Windowing System

Within TCP/IP is support for a windowing system. It is not similar to Microsoft Windows, but it appears to be. The way it works is entirely different. This windowing system is based on the X protocol, which sits on top of TCP.

This windowing system is different from Microsoft Windows if for no other reason than it supports programs running on different machines in a windowing environment.

2.2 What Is Client and Server?

I remember when I began working with TCP/IP; my first question was, "What is a TELNET?" I was not to the point of worrying about a client or server. So if you are new to TCP/IP, you may be asking yourself the same question. This is understandable and focusing upon this first will orient you to greater detail later.

The terms client and server have risen from virtual obscurity not more than a half dozen years ago to headlines in many trade magazines and weeklies today (at the time of this writing). In many instances the use of the terms defies explanation beyond some nebulous idea that is attempted to be conveyed.

For example, I read articles constantly where the terms client/server are used, and the only ascertainable meaning I can derive from them is that a peer relationship exists between something. The point is these terms take on connotations usually contingent upon the vendor. However, with TCP/IP this is not the case; they mean something specific and definable.

In TCP/IP three popular applications exist. They are actually part of the TCP/IP stack, assuming the TCP/IP stack is coded against what is considered the baseline for TCP/IP. These applications are:

1. TELNET

2. File Transfer Protocol (FTP)

3. Simple Mail Transfer Protocol (SMTP)

All three of these applications can be divided into two parts. These two parts are a client and a server. Understanding their operation is easy. With respect to the TCP/IP applications mentioned above one must only remember two things to master the concept of client/server. Clients always invoke (start) a process. Servers always "serve" a client's request.

For example, if a user on system "A" enters TELNET B, the TELNET client gets invoked from the TCP/IP stack on system "A." Then, system "A's" client will be expecting system "B's" TELNET server to answer the requests of the client. Consider figure 2.2.

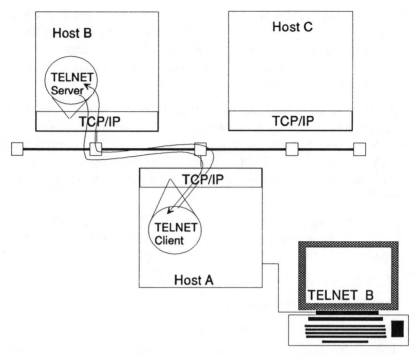

Figure 2.2

Notice in figure 2.2 each host has a TCP/IP stack on it. Also, each machine is attached to a Bus backbone via a transceiver. Within the arena of TCP/IP networking, each node (any device attached to the network) must have TCP/IP loaded onto it for that device to function with other devices on the network.

Not all devices require complete TCP/IP stacks. Some have complement stacks because the device performs a specific function and does not require a complete TCP/IP protocol stack to operate with other devices on the network. An example of this could be a communications server used to connect modems to a TCP/IP network.

Figure 2.2 depicted an example of a TELNET client and server, but the same holds true for FTP and SMTP. That means when a user enters FTP and a target host name, against a TCP/IP stack, an FTP client gets invoked and attempts to establish a logical connection with the destination FTP server. The same is true for SMTP, except the names are different.

This is client/server in respect to TCP/IP. Yes, a peer concept exists, but beyond the generalization of this concept are specifics in the TCP/IP networking protocols. Additional details about the function of clients/servers will be presented later.

2.3 How Can TCP/IP Work with Different Operating Systems?

Good question! This is possible because it was originally conceived and developed over time to be software and hardware independent. TCP/IP software itself must be modified to operate with different operating systems. This means vendors manufacturing/supporting operating systems must customize TCP/IP software to the particular operating system it is to operate under.

Explaining this another way would include envisioning TCP/IP in respect to layers of where "stuff" is on any given machine. Consider figure 2.3.

General Computer Components by Layer

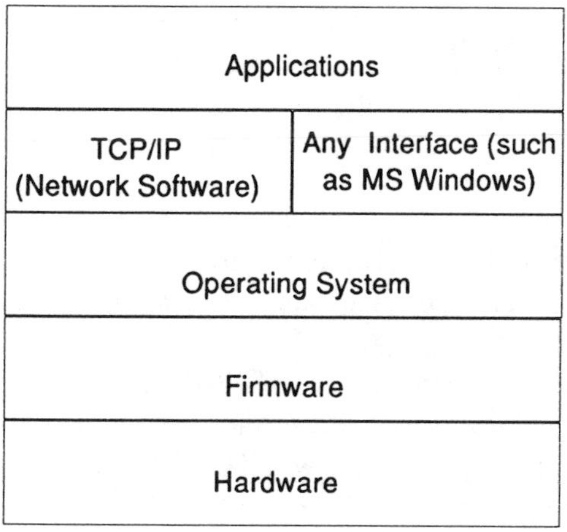

Applications	
TCP/IP (Network Software)	Any Interface (such as MS Windows)
Operating System	
Firmware	
Hardware	

Figure 2.3

Granted figure 2.3 is a generalization, but it does depict how major components appear in relation to TCP/IP.

In contrast to TCP/IP are other network protocols. These type network protocols are considered proprietary because they operate on certain vendor equipment. They are not "open" in the sense another vendor can manipulate the protocol to operate on its equipment and maintain the native nature of the proprietary protocol.

2.4 Are All TCP/IP Protocol Stacks Alike?

No. The Data Defense Network (DDN) manuals and other documents are considered official TCP/IP standards. Because of the open nature of TCP/IP different vendors have put varying twists on TCP/IP protocol stacks. Where I have seen this to be the case, it was typically to support some particular "thing" the vendor wanted to do. It is not inherently bad or good, but buyers of TCP/IP products should ask how close is the particular product to the official TCP/IP standards.

TCP/IP is generally considered open and not owned by any company or standards making body. This is true, but TCP/IP components and general direction is guided by different groups and agencies that serve more of a steering role than a mandating one.

2.5 Conclusion

Networks can be built with different network protocols. TCP/IP is a network protocol that is popular today. It is mature in the sense that it has been in circulation (operation) for many years now. As a result, it has become relatively inexpensive. TCP/IP's past has been rooted in governmental agencies, universities, and other noncorporate entities. But, because of the explosive growth TCP/IP has experienced in the corporate community worldwide in the past half dozen years, it has come to the forefront of many networking conversations. Many users (the nontechnocrats) have not had exposure to TCP/IP generally because of its lack of presence in the corporate community. Only in the past fifteen to twenty years has the computer explosion occurred, and it's easy to understand why a lack of knowledge exists about TCP/IP and many other topics.

TCP/IP is a client/server technology at the application layer. In TCP/IP, clients always invoke a process and servers always serve the request of clients. Other references are prevalent today using the terms client/server, usually to indicate something peer oriented.

TCP/IP was originally conceived and has been continually refined to be software and hardware independent. Originally, TCP/IP was intended to be the glue in a network to connect heterogeneous devices. To that end it has had a long and continuing, prosperous life. TCP/IP must be modified to operate with various operating systems, but a consensus exists to modify it only so it can operate with a different operating system, thus leaving the fundamental characteristics of it intact.

Not all TCP/IP protocol stacks are what they seem. Because of the robust design and flexibility inherent in TCP/IP, developers who sell it can customize it to provide certain services. This is not necessarily good or bad. The point is that buyers should understand what is generally considered standard TCP/IP. Being able to recognize any variation that might exist is important; it can make the difference between a smooth implementation and an unpleasant surprise when performance is not consistent with expectations.

Chapter 3

TCP/IP: An Overview

Now comes the history lesson! TCP/IP is a set of network protocols that work at upper layers in a network. TCP/IP is referred to as a protocol suite and sometimes a protocol stack (as it is loosely known). TCP/IP has been shrouded in misunderstanding about its origins, related entities and organizations, and implementations. It evolved over a span of two decades and is not owned by any vendor or professional organization that serves as a standard making body. However, the United States Department of Defense (DoD) provides some oversight to maintain a semblance of order.

This chapter presents a basic technical overview of TCP/IP. A brief history of the origins of TCP/IP is presented. Also, TCP/IP components in respect to layers are explained. A correlation is made between network layers and associated TCP/IP names and or addresses that apply aid in understanding TCP/IP as a whole. A section on the Internet is presented and explained. An internet is explained and contrasted with the Internet. A term frequently used in conjunction with TCP/IP is ETHERNET. Its role is explained. A summary wraps up the highlights of topics presented.

3.1 TCP/IP History

TCP/IP origins are in a governmental organization called the Advanced Research Project Agency (ARPA) dating back to the '60s. ARPA, a Department of Defense (DoD) agency, conducted research and experiments in search of a solution to provide interoperability between different computer equipment. ARPANET was the result and was operational in 1969. ARPANET eventually expanded across the country and formed the main network of what began to be called the Internet.

The Defense Advanced Research Project Agency (DARPA) succeeded ARPA in 1971, thus ARPANET was under their domain. DARPA focused on research and experiments using packet-switching technology emphasizing satellite and radio technology for transport mechanisms.

In 1975 the Defense Communications Agency (DCA) took responsibility for ARPANET operation. About this time a new set of networking protocols had been proposed. These protocols laid the foundation for TCP/IP, and by 1978 TCP/IP had become stable enough for a demonstration. TCP/IP contributed to the growth in the number of networks located around the country and consequently an increase of networks connected to ARPANET.

In 1982 DoD created the Defense Data Network (DDN) and designated it as the focal point for distributed networks comprising the Internet. Shortly after this (in 1983), DoD stated acceptance of TCP/IP as the protocol that nodes should use to connect to the Internet. This statement of acceptance of TCP/IP ignited explosive growth of TCP/IP networks because now a recommended network protocol existed with the sole intent to permit interoperability between different vendor computers. TCP/IP continued to grow in universities, government organizations, and other places providing many people with exposure to TCP/IP.

Local Area Network (LAN) growth in the '80s contributed to additional TCP/IP growth. LANs were easily installed and could be expanded as requirements increased. TCP/IP growth profited from mergers and acquisitions that swept the business community. To a certain degree TCP/IP seemed to be the natural "link" that could bring together different companies' computer systems, and by the end of the '80s TCP/IP had become a dominant networking force throughout the world.

3.2 TCP/IP Components

Application Layer Components

TCP/IP was architected machine independent and is a client/server technology at the application layer. A client initiates (invokes) an application, and servers serve the requests of clients. Because of TCP/IP's design, TELNET (the application for remote logons) has a client and server, just as FTP (the application used for file transfers), and SMTP (the application used for E-Mail). Notice figure 3.1 where TELNET, FTP, SMTP, and other services reside at the application level.

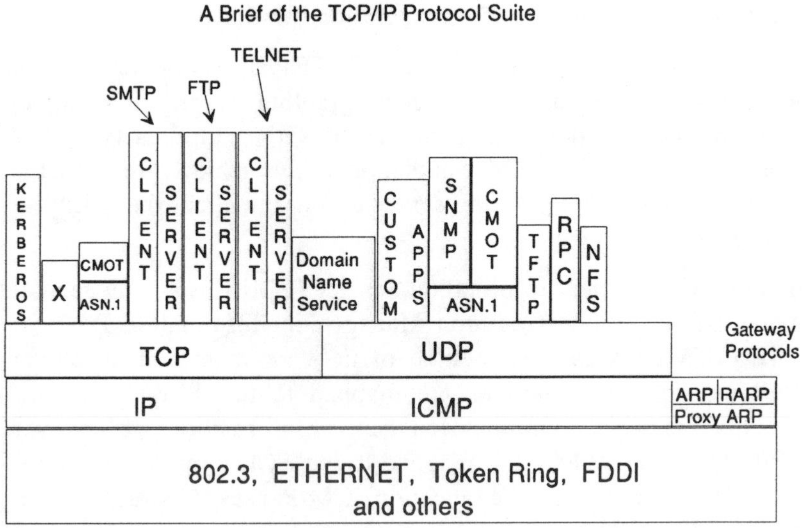

A Brief of the TCP/IP Protocol Suite

Figure 3.1

Other application layer components exist. X is a protocol and provides a distributed window environment. It permits requests-responses between X client applications and an X server. X includes the ability of an X client executing on one machine to operate against an X server on another machine, thus enabling a distributed windowing environment. Some X basic components include:

- X Server—A program providing display services on a terminal supporting graphics at the request of an X client application.

- X Client—A program using the services provided by an X Server, such as a terminal emulation for example.

- X Window Manager—This program helps in resizing windows, modifying windows, and relocating windows.

- X Library—This contains the interface for application programming. It consists of C language subroutines. One function of the XLIB is to convert X client requests into X protocol requests.

- X Toolkits—This is a software library providing high level facilities for implementing buttons, menus, etc.

- Widgets—A widget is an X window, additional data, and procedures used to perform operations on that data.

Kerberos is a security protocol used with TCP/IP that operates by an authentication server, and by a "ticket" granting server. For example, a client requests a "ticket" to meet the "ticket" granting server, thus achieving authentication. Once authentication is achieved the ticket is presented to the ticket granting server giving the client the ability to use a particular service.

Common Management Information Service (CMIS) is a management service offered by the Common Management Information Protocol (CMIP). CMIP is an OSI method of network management. When CMIP management functions are mapped to the TCP/IP suite of protocols it is called Common Management Information Service over TCP/IP (CMOT). When it is mapped to the TCP/IP protocol suite it uses TCP for a transport connection. CMIP uses Abstract Syntax Notation 1 (ASN.1), a language defined by Internet standard documents. ASN.1 is a language for writing clear and uniform datatype definitions used in the management function.

Simple Network Management Protocol (SNMP) uses UDP for a transport mechanism. Instead of the terms client/server, SNMP uses the terms managers and agents. Agents maintain information about the status of the node. A manager (application) communicates with agents throughout the network via messages. This information about the status of a device is maintained in a Management Information Base MIB.

Remote Procedure Calls (RPCs) are programs permitting applications to call a routine executing a server; in turn the server returns variables and return codes to the requester. Simply, it is a mechanism implemented to support distributed computing via a client/server model.

Network File Server (NFS) is a collection of protocols produced by SUN MicroSystems that uses a distributed file system allowing multiple computers supporting NFS to access each others' directories transparently.

Trivial File Transfer Protocol (TFTP) uses UDP; it has no security such as FTP that utilizes TCP as a transport mechanism. It is a very simple means of file transfer and not robust when compared to FTP.

Domain Name Service, also called the Domain Name System (DNS), is a distributed database system of IP addresses and aliases. It resolves addresses of hosts in order to establish contact with the target host. DNS was created to solve the problem of maintaining a host file on each host participating in a TCP/IP network. A host file consists of IP addresses and aliases, and each time a host or network is added or taken away the host file needs changing. DNS was designed to forego the constant updating of each host file on every host.

Transport Layer Components

Two different transport mechanisms are part of TCP/IP, Transmission Control Protocol (TCP) and User Datagram Protocol (UDP). TCP is connection-oriented, providing retransmissions and reliable data transfer. It manages data passed down to it from the application layer from the perspective of maintaining a reliable transport mechanism.

UDP is connectionless-oriented, it does not provide retransmissions or guarantee reliable data transfer. UDP is used by custom written programs for specific purposes. These programs are individually responsible for insuring reliable data transfer (checking to see if the data arrived at the destined location) and retransmissions (repeating a transmission of data due to a loss caused by some type problem).

Network Layer Protocols

Internet Protocol (IP) transports datagrams across a network. A datagram consists of the data from the application layer and the transport level header and trailer information. IP resides at network layer three. It uses a 32 bit addressing scheme whereby the network and host are identified. IP was originally designed to accommodate routers and hosts produced by different vendors.

Internet Control Message Protocol (ICMP) provides messages concerning the status of nodes. These messages may reflect an error that has occurred or simply the status of a node. ICMP provides a way for certain commands to be issued against a target host to determine the status of the host, such as Packet Internet Groper (PING). ICMP and IP are implemented together because of how the two are intertwined in the routing and response mechanisms.

Address Resolution Protocol (ARP) determines the physical address (sometimes called a hard address) of a node given that node's IP address. ARP is the mapping link between IP addresses and the underlying physical address, for example, the ETHERNET address. It is via ARP that a logical connection (BIND) occurs between the IP address and the hard address.

Reverse Address Resolution Protocol (RARP) enables a host to discover its own IP address by broadcasting its physical address. When the broadcast occurs another node on the LAN answers back with the IP address of the requesting node. Hence, it is commonly called reverse ARP.

Gateway Protocols are a collection of protocols that allow routers to communicate. A variety of them exist; an example would be Routing Information Protocol (RIP). RIP is a basic protocol used to exchange information between routers. Again, this is a misnomer now because gateways are network devices performing a specific function which is usually not routing. Open Shortest Path First (OSPF) is another.

Data Link Layer Protocols

TCP/IP does not define data link level protocols. This is due to TCP/IP's original design intent. As stated in chapter 1, TCP/IP can use different types of data link layer protocols including:

- ETHERNET
- Token Ring
- Fiber Distributed Data Interface (FDDI)
- X.25

Media Implementations

TCP/IP can be found implemented with multiple types of media. For example, if TCP/IP is implemented with ETHERNET, media could be coaxial cable or copper stranded cable. TCP/IP can also operate with fiber optic media. If TCP/IP is implemented using X.25, then satellite, microwave, or serial telephone type lines may be the media used.

3.3 The Internet

The word "Internet" has been a point of confusion in the marketplace. "Internet" was the name used to refer to ARPANET with other networks connected to it. The Internet has grown, and ARPANET remained the main network of the Internet until the late '80s when it was replaced by the National Science Foundation Network (NSFNET). The primary purpose for the change was the need to incorporate high speed links in various places.

The Internet has a greater role than military usage, but DoD maintains coordination of it. The DDN Network Information Center (NIC) maintains what are known as Request for Comments (RFCs). These are protocol descriptions, ideas, and other comments from individuals interested in the Internet, and in a real sense this is part of what makes TCP/IP public domain. Individual RFCs have a state and status assigned to them. RFC states include:

- Standard
- Draft
- Proposal
- Experiment

RFC's status include:

- Required
- Recommended
- Elective
- Limited Use
- Not Recommended

3.4 The internet

An internet is a locally administered LAN utilizing TCP/IP for its upper layer protocols. It does not have all of the restrictions and requirements the Internet must abide by because it is a "local" network. But, an internet does have restrictions and requirements in order for it to be functional.

Many globally connected internets connect to the Internet. Special restrictions apply to internets connected to the Internet. Typically, the connection of individual internets to the Internet must be accomplished by having a multihomed host—a host attached to two or more LANs. A multihomed host connecting an internet to the Internet has a local internet address and an Internet address assigned to it so it can be known by both networks.

3.5 ETHERNET's Role with TCP/IP

ETHERNET is a term often used in conjunction with TCP/IP. It is a data link level protocol and a broadcast technology. The ETHERNET specification does specify cable requirements and other specifications. ETHERNET is implemented in computer systems and devices by firmware on a network interface card (NIC). The name ETHERNET came from a theoretical electromagnetic material named "luminiferous ether." This material was thought to be a universal element holding together the universe and its parts! The leap of reason was an "ETHER"-net could be a link to bind all components connected to the network.

The Xerox corporation started a research facility in Palo Alto, California, in 1970, called Palo Alto Research Center (PARC). Commissioned with the task of charting a course towards what Xerox thought would be an electronic office in the 1990s, PARC devoted time, talent, and teams to envision where Xerox would make its next market since it already had a strong foothold in copying machines, etc.

In 1973 PARC had a team working on networking computers, printers, and other devices. Specifically, a man by the name of Robert Metcalfe worked with a team to find a way to speed up the link between computers and printers on the network. They created a way to connect computers and printers on a network whereby higher speeds could be achieved than what was used in the past. This is what would become known as ETHERNET. Prior to ETHERNET the technology of the day required fifteen minutes to transmit and print a page with a resolution of 600 dots per inch. The first implementation of ETHERNET cut this fifteen-minute time period down to seconds; it was a major breakthrough and got a lot of attention. This version of ETHERNET was later known as experimental ETHERNET and had a data transfer rate of approximately 2.6 megabits per second. Time passed, and in 1982 Digital Equipment Corporation, Intel, and Xerox presented Version 2.0 ETHERNET, which specified 10 megabits per second data transfer rate, among other specifications.

ETHERNET and TCP/IP are different technologies, but together they create an effective LAN. ETHERNET is a protocol and operates at layers one and two in a network. TCP/IP is a suite of protocols and operates at network layers three and above. ETHERNET has a 48 bit addressing scheme and uses it to communicate with other ETHERNET NICs. TCP/IP uses IP's 32 bit addressing to identify networks and hosts. ETHERNET and TCP/IP can operate together because of a protocol that is a part of TCP/IP, namely Address Resolution Protocol (ARP). ARP maps ETHERNET addresses to IP addresses and vice versa.

By the end of the '80s, ETHERNET, like TCP/IP, could be bought off the shelf at computer stores. ETHERNET and TCP/IP's maturity as a technology and their inexpensive price make them a good match for a networking solution. These characteristics and others have contributed to the dominance of TCP/IP based ETHERNET LANs.

3.6 Conclusion

TCP/IP is a mature networking protocol dating back to the 1970s. Its proliferation among universities, government institutions, and organizations of all types has contributed to its dominance in the marketplace. TCP/IP is best defined as an evolving network protocol with core components capable of networking heterogeneous hosts. TCP/IP's power lies in the following:

- It can operate on different vendor computers.
- Remote logons, file transfers, and electronic mail are three major applications it provides.

- Its IP addressing scheme makes connecting multiple networks relatively easy.
- It offers two distinct transport mechanisms.
- It has relatively low overhead from the standpoint of amount of software code required to provide a particular function.
- It is relatively inexpensive.
- A broad base of technical people have experience with it.
- It can operate with multiple data link level protocols and different types of media.

TCP/IP is based on a client/server relationship at an application layer. This client/server technology makes its applications fundamentally user friendly. Other components make up TCP/IP including network management and a distributed windowing mechanism.

Associated with TCP/IP are the Internet and the internet. The Internet (big I) is comprised of the NFSNET and other networks connected to it making a virtual network spanning the globe. The internet (little i) is what is implemented in locally administered environments. Institutions, businesses, organizations, and even individuals can connect to the (big I) Internet.

A term frequently heard when TCP/IP is discussed is ETHERNET. Created at PARC, refined by Digital, Intel, and Xerox, ETHERNET has become the common data link level protocol used with TCP/IP networks. A broadcast technology and capable of being implemented over different types of media, ETHERNET has permeated the marketplace. It is mature and inexpensive, and this has also contributed to its success.

Together TCP/IP and ETHERNET are a good choice to provide LAN services. Both accommodate the novice and the network technocrat. Together they provide not only networking basics but also the foundation to exploit advanced networking techniques including distributed databases, network management, and even file systems. Their proven effectiveness continues to make them a network of choice for many implementers.

Chapter 4

What Is a TELNET?

This chapter begins our focus upon popular TCP/IP applications. We start with TELNET because of its popularity in the TCP/IP protocol stack. This chapter explores what TELNET is, the concept of a raw TELNET, how TELNET is used, valid TELNET commands, helpful hints when using TELNET, and what a TN3270 client is compared and contrasted to a raw TELNET.

Some of you may be asking, "What is a TELNET anyway?" "How do I use it?" "What does it do?" And, "What are the commands used with it?" These questions are common for those new to TCP/IP and particularly TELNET.

4.1 What Is TELNET?

TELNET is an application that provides logon capabilities to remote systems. It consists of two parts as shown in figure 4.1.

The TCP/IP Protocol Suite

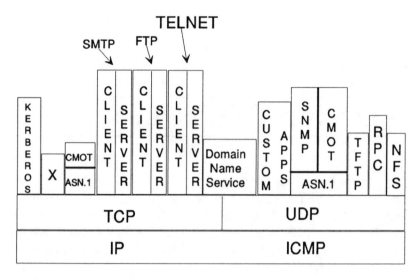

Figure 4.1

Why are remote logon capabilities important? Well, in a network environment a fundamental idea behind it is sharing resources. This implies multiple computers and related devices connected together in such a manner that access from multiple sources is possible. In order for a user on any given computer to access resources on another computer requires a remote logon capability. This is what TELNET does.

For example, consider a small network with three computers. Let us assume each computer has a primary purpose. Computer "A" is a machine dedicated for training. It has training programs on it that anyone on the network can use. Computer "B" is a machine used to archive customer files; it has a large database running on it. Computer "C" has users connected to it performing interactive tasks. This means users are directly attached to computer "C" and they do most of their work on this machine. But because of the network, users on machine "C" have access to computers "A" and "B." Consider figure 4.2.

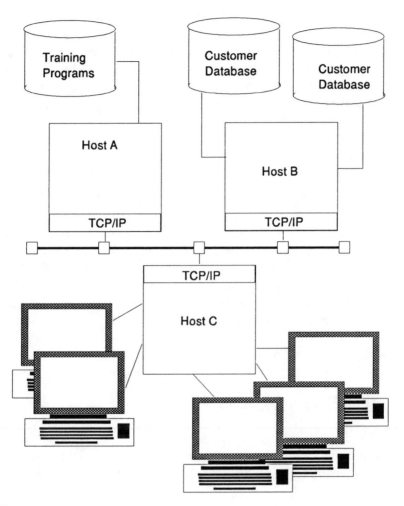

Figure 4.2

Notice the computers in figure 4.2 have TCP/IP on each of them and they are all connected to a common medium. So, for users on computer "C" to access a training program on computer "A," the user on computer "C" would type TELNET A at the command prompt on computer "C."

Once the user on computer "C" enters the TELNET A command, the TELNET client gets invoked on computer "C." After the TELNET client is invoked it examines a file commonly known as /etc/hosts (particularly UNIX based computers) searching for a device name "A." Assuming it finds it, it then examines its corresponding internet address as the computer is known to all TCP/IP software. Next, sparing much detail, the TELNET server located on machine "A" answers the client's request (from computer "C") for a logical connection to be established. It is, and then the logon prompt from computer "A" is displayed on the user's terminal connected to computer "C."

Another possibility for what a TELNET client does once it gets invoked is quite common in many networks. It interacts with what is called a Domain Name Resolver. The Domain Name Resolver works by a database that maintains device names and internet addresses on networks. When employed, TELNET clients use this instead of the typical /etc/hosts file to find the address for the target host. The reason behind this is efficiency. In large networks the Domain Name System is used. The consequence if a Domain Name System is not used in a network is that all /etc/hosts files and other pertinent files must be updated anytime new hosts are added to the network.

4.2 TELNET Characteristics

TELNET is an application and a protocol. From an application perspective, TELNET provides the ability for a user to invoke it and perform a remote logon with another host as shown in figure 4.3

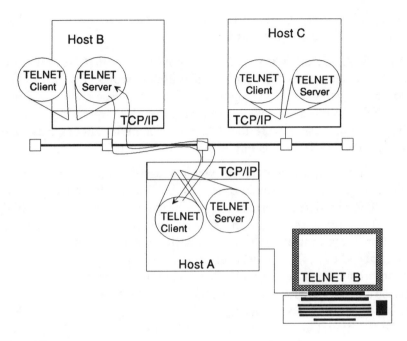

Figure 4.3

Figure 4.3 shows the TELNET client on host "A" requesting a logical connection with the TELNET server in host "B." The important thing to observe is both TELNET client and server are part of the TCP/IP stack on each network device.

A Raw TELNET

Figure 4.3 depicts three hosts with a TCP/IP stack, each with a native TELNET client and server. It also shows a user invoking a TELNET client from the TCP/IP protocol stack on the computer "A" by entering TELNET at an operating system prompt. In many technical circles this use of TELNET client is referred to as a raw TELNET; specifically referring to the TELNET client. The TELNET client is considered native because the TELNET client is inherent to the TCP/IP protocol stack.

Since TELNET is also protocol, additional explanation is in order. So far focus has been upon the TELNET application. But the TELNET protocol can be used to create a program called a TN3270 Client

Application. Operational differences exist between a raw TELNET client and a TN3270 client application.

A raw TELNET client is popular for logons to hosts that use ASCII for data representation. For example, if a user is working on a Convex computer (using the UNIX operating system), he/she can issue a raw TELNET against a SUN computer (using the UNIX operating system). Both systems use ASCII for data representation. This is a typical scenario where TCP/IP is implemented and TELNET is used.

A different requirement exists when a user needs to log on to a computer that uses Extended Binary Coded Decimal Interchange Code (EBCDIC) for data representation and the source computer uses ASCII for data representation. In today's heterogeneous networking environments a variety of hosts (with different operating systems) may be attached to any given network, particularly TCP/IP. Assume three hosts are attached to a network. Assume two of these hosts are UNIX based and use ASCII data representation by default. Assume one of the hosts is an IBM system using the VM operating system and it has TCP/IP operating on it. The VM host uses EBCDIC data representation by default. Figure 4.4 depicts such an example.

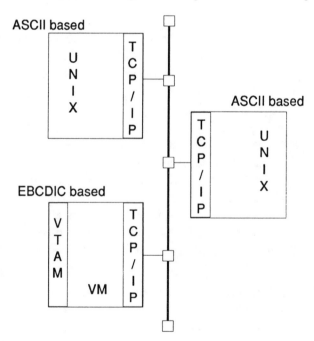

Figure 4.4

Figure 4.4 shows hosts that use different methods of representing data; two use ASCII and one uses EBCDIC. In figure 4.5 two UNIX hosts and one VM host are present. All hosts are connected to the same network and use TCP/IP as the network protocol.

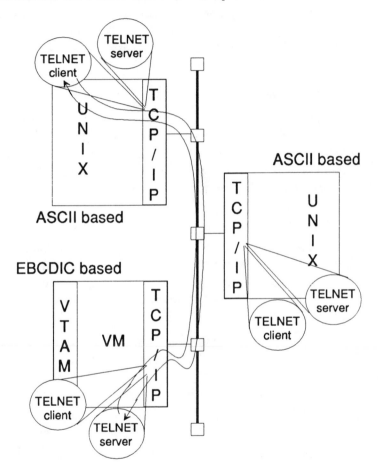

Figure 4.5

In figure 4.5 the TELNET client is invoked on a UNIX (ASCII based host) and the TELNET server in the TCP/IP stack on the VM machine answers the request of the client. Additionally, the TCP/IP stack on the VM machine performs protocol conversion. This means that TCP/IP protocol is converted to SNA on the VM machine. It also performs translation (ASCII-to-EBCDIC and vice versa outbound from the VM machine).

In summary, figure 4.5 shows the VM machine performing two functions. It performs protocol conversion and data translation. However, with the appropriate product, data translation can be performed on the UNIX host and, consequently, over time realize savings when measured by CPU cycles. This is done with a TN3270 client.

TN3270 Client Application

A TELNET protocol is defined, and if an individual with required knowledge wishes to design a program based on TELNET protocol, they can. The most common program written using TELNET protocol is an emulator application providing data translation services between ASCII and EBCDIC and vice versa. This program (application) is called a TN3270 client.

TELNET (within a native TCP/IP protocol stack) typically uses ASCII based data, and it does not fit into SNA natively, which is dominated by EBCDIC. In the SNA world, the EBCDIC goes a step further and defines what are called data streams. A few specific data streams exist, but a dominant one is the 3270 data stream. It is used with terminals and printers.

Because of the difference in ASCII and EBCDIC, converting ASCII into EBCDIC, specifically into a 3270 or a 5250 data stream, is required. The question is where will this process take place. With the data stream dilemma between TCP/IP networks and SNA networks, this fundamental issue must be resolved.

So, how do users on a TCP/IP based network have ASCII data converted into the EBCDIC? Two possible solutions exist.

First, a raw TELNET client can be used to establish a logical connection between a UNIX or other non-EBCDIC host and an EBCDIC based host. If this is the case, then ASCII to EBCDIC translation will occur on the EBCDIC host (with the exception of when a gateway is used between the two and translation services are provided or other scenarios).

Second, a TN3270 client application can be used like a raw TELNET to gain entry into the SNA environment, but a TN3270 client application performs data translation. This means it sends an EBCDIC (3270 or 5250 data stream to the destination host). The point is the TN3270 client application translates ASCII data into an EBCDIC; that being a 3270 or 5250 data stream. Figure 4.6 shows two UNIX hosts and a VM host connected to a network. On one UNIX host a TN3270 client application exists.

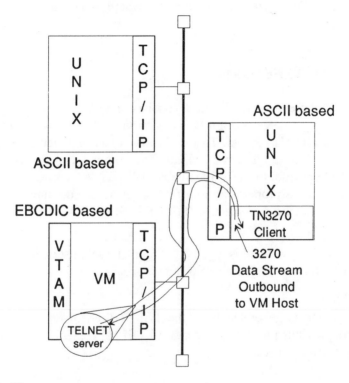

Figure 4.6

In figure 4.6, the TN3270 client is shown establishing a logical connection with the telnet server native to the TCP/IP protocol on the VM machine. But, notice in figure 4.6 the data stream leaving the ASCII based host is EBCDIC! Magic? No, it works because data format (be it ASCII or EBCDIC) gets formatted at layer six within a network. By the time "the data" gets down to the interface card connecting it to the network, "the data" is represented by voltages or light pulses, whichever the network is based upon.

The net effect of having TN3270 clients is that they do pay for themselves over a period of time if used in a scenario such as figure 4.6. But, there are many instances where they (TN3270 applications) are not needed and provide little if any benefit to the end user. Both a raw TELNET and a TN3270 client provide the user with remote logon capability. Both the raw TELNET and TN3270 client are client applications. The difference is merely where data translation is performed.

4.3   How Is TELNET Used?

As mentioned previously, TELNET consists of a client and server. A client always initiates a logical connection and a server always answers the client's request. To use TELNET, a command must be entered to invoke the TELNET client. The command to invoke the TELNET client from the TCP/IP suite is TELNET. Assuming TCP/IP has been installed properly and normal setup occurred, entering the TELNET command invokes the TELNET client from the TCP/IP protocol stack.

If the TELNET command is entered without a target host name, alias, or internet address, the following prompt appears:

    telnet>

This command is generated from the TELNET client on that host. When the previous prompt appears, valid TELNET client commands can be entered against it.

4.4   What Are Valid TELNET Client Commands?

Valid TELNET client commands can be entered at the TELNET client prompt. If a user does not know valid commands to execute against a TELNET client prompt, a question mark can be entered (?) and a list of valid TELNET commands will be displayed. An abbreviated list of valid TELNET client commands and a brief explanation of each is listed:

close—This closes a current connection if one is established.

display—This command will display the operating parameters in use for TELNET. Because these parameters can be changed, they are site dependent.

mode—This command indicates whether entry can be made line-by-line or one-character-at-a-time mode.

open—This command is required prior to the target host name in order for session establishment to occur.

quit—This command is entered to exit the telnet> prompt, thus exiting TELNET.

send—In certain instances special characters may need to be transmitted. This provides the means to accommodate some of these characters.

set—This command is used to set certain parameters to be enforced during a TELNET session.

status—This command provides information regarding the connection and any operating parameters in force for the TELNET session.

toggle—This command is used to toggle (change) operating parameters.

z—This command will suspend the telnet> prompt.

?—This command prints valid TELNET commands that can be entered against the telnet> prompt.

4.5 Helpful Hints Using TELNET

Using TELNET is fairly straightforward. Once users break through the newness of the technology it is not difficult. Learning TELNET is easier when one understands basic TELNET operation, TELNET commands, and how to log on to hosts appropriately.

Since TELNET is part of the TCP/IP protocol suite it does work with other components in the suite. For example, if one attempts to establish a remote logon with a target host, and after a period of time a response is displayed on the terminal something to the effect "host unreachable" or some other message, this indicates problems are not necessarily related to TELNET. In this example, the "host unreachable" message comes from the Internet Control Message Protocol (ICMP) component. This is an integral part of the IP layer. It provides messages responding to different conditions. Here, a destination host is not reachable by the TELNET client. The obvious question is, why? With this example a couple of possible reasons would be viable. It could be the host is unreachable because of a break in the network connection. Or, it could be that the host is located on another segment of the network and for some reason, inaccessible at the moment. Other possibilities exist.

When messages such as these appear they are most often generated from the ICMP portion of the TCP/IP suite. It would be helpful to familiarize yourself with common messages and understand their meaning. It can prove to be a valuable troubleshooting tool.

4.6 Conclusion

TELNET is a very popular application in the TCP/IP protocol suite. It provides remote logon capabilities. It operates on a client/server method of communication. Each TELNET, native to the majority of TCP/IP protocol stacks, consists of a client and server. A client is used to initiate a request. Servers always respond to the request of a client.

TELNET is both an application and a protocol. It is an application in its native sense. It is also a protocol in its native sense; they are not diametrically opposed. The TELNET protocol can be used to write a TN3270 client application.

A TN3270 client application provides a user with the advantage of performing data translation on the host where the TN3270 client resides. To use a TN3270 client application requires communication with a TELNET server. This may be a TELNET server in a TCP/IP stack on an EBCDIC host, or it may be a customized program called a TN3270 server. The latter does little more than provide the necessary ability to establish a logical connection with a TN3270 client.

Chapter 5

What Is FTP?

File Transfer Protocol (FTP) is a popular application providing a means whereby files can be transferred (actually copied) from any host implementing TCP/IP to any other host implementing TCP/IP, or required components therein. Files are not transferred in the sense they are removed from a system, rather a file is copied from the source host to the destination host. The original file is neither moved nor changed, only read.

FTP is considered a user application and is fairly easy to use. It is like TELNET in that it has a client and server which constitute the FTP application. The FTP client is used to initiate a file transfer and the FTP server is used to serve FTP client requests, thus making the logical connection between the client and server. Consider figure 5.1.

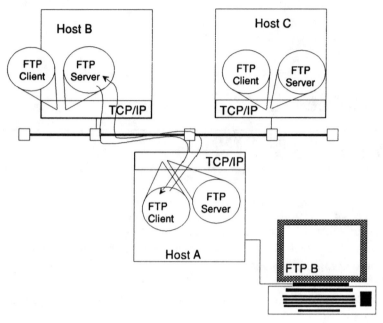

Figure 5.1

Most hosts that have a TCP/IP protocol suite have FTP (which consists of a client and server).

5.1 What Basic Functions Can FTP Perform?

The following lists basic functions available with FTP.

- The ability to copy a single file from one host to another. Consider figure 5.2

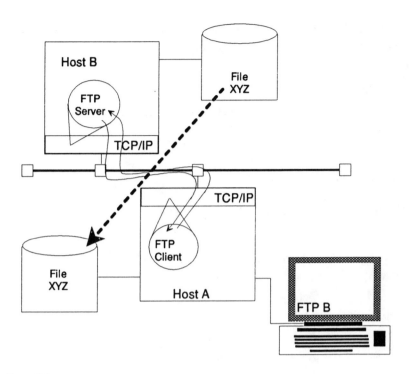

Figure 5.2

Figure 5.2 shows the XYZ file copied from host B to host A. The display on host A shows the FTP client being invoked to establish the session.

- The ability to copy multiple files from one host to another host
- The ability to list all accessible files in a target host
- The capability to create and/or remove directories in a target host
- The ability to identify the current directory in a target host
- The ability to append a local file to a file located in a remote (target) host
- The ability to append a file from a local host to a file located in a target host

In addition to providing these functions, commands can be executed against an FTP client. When the prompt below is present, an FTP client has been invoked:

ftp>

A number of commands are executable against the FTP client. Section 5.2 lists some of those commonly used.

5.2 FTP Commands

The following lists valid FTP commands:

!	dir	mode	rmdir
$	disconnect	mput	runique
account	form	nmap	send
append	get	ntrans	sendport
ascii	glob	open	status
bell	hash	prompt	struct
binary	help	proxy	sunique
bye	lcd	put	tenex
case	ls	pwd	trace
cd	macdef	quit	type
cdup	mdelete	quote	user
close	mdir	recv	verbose
cr	mget	remotehelp	?
debug	mkdir	rename	
delete	mls	reset	

Most of these commands need no examination (and some do!), but to orient you to the commands, some popular ones are examined here:

get—This command is issued against an FTP client to "get" a file from the target machine. It copies the file rather than removing it.

put—This command enables a user to "put" a file from the source host from which the FTP client was invoked to the target (destination) host. It copies the file rather than removing it as well.

open—If FTP> is displayed and "open" is issued, the FTP client will prompt the user for the target host name.

close—When FTP> is displayed, this command terminates the logical connection between the source and destination host.

Most of the commands that can be issued against the FTP client are fairly intuitive. The list itself is typical of FTP commands which could be obtained from most FTP client prompts. Other commands may well exist with TCP/IP stacks from other vendors.

5.3   How to Use Some Popular FTP Commands

To start a logical connection with FTP, a user would issue FTP at the operating system prompt. Assuming configuration has been performed properly, the following would appear:

    ftp>

Many users issue FTP and a host name or an appropriate address with it. For example, FTP RISC6000.

All following commands are issued against the FTP client prompt.

user—Prompts for a user id, then password.

quote—Displays the operating parameters of the target host.

ls—Lists the files in the working directory of the target host. It is like performing a directory listing command against the directory of the target host.

mkdir—Permits a user to create a directory on the target host.

ascii—Places FTP in ASCII mode for file transfers.

binary—Causes binary file transfer.

quit—Terminates FTP client.

When performing file transfers, messages appear on the display at different times. For example, after a user has established an FTP session the ftp> prompt is present. If a user enters "get" and a valid filename on the target host, messages will be displayed stating the status of the connection. Messages will also reflect the internet and port address, name of the file being received, size of the file, and the time it took for file transfer (copying) to take place.

5.4 What Is the Mystery Behind FTP?

There is none. It is simply a file transfer mechanism that enables users to transfer (copy) file(s) from one machine to another. In many ways its simplicity is its complexity. Commands like put and get, open and close, do what they imply; but other commands are not that intuitive. In some instances commands can be customized, depending upon the vendors' implementation of the TCP/IP stack.

The ease of use behind FTP is the fact it operates the same on virtually any machine. Once TELNET, FTP, and other native applications and functions are invoked their operation is the same regardless of the operating system or hardware platform.

5.5 Conclusion

FTP is a user application for file transfer (copying) of files from any machine with TCP/IP to another machine with TCP/IP. Exceptions to this are when integration occurs and heterogeneous networks are connected. To implement an FTP server (or FTP client) on an MVS, VM, or VSE host does not necessarily require a complete TCP/IP protocol stack on that machine.

A variety of commands can be issued against FTP. Those listed here will help readers new to this topic. No mystery exists with FTP. It operates in a straightforward fashion. Normally, it is the newness of TCP/IP applications and the accompanying acronyms that tend to create some initial discomfort with new users. However, this is the case with practically any networking protocol that is new to a user.

Chapter 6

What Is SMTP?

Simple Mail Transfer Protocol (SMTP) is part of the TCP/IP suite of protocols. It is a mechanism for electronic mail transfer. The concept of sender and receiver is used with SMTP and is parallel to the client/server relationship used in TELNET and FTP.

6.1 SMTP Components

Electronic mail is fairly simple in concept and operation. Its basic structure appears like figure 6.1.

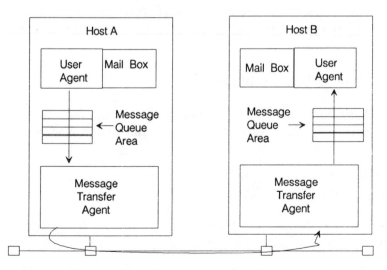

Figure 6.1

Figure 6.1 shows two hosts connected to a network. Each host has the same components for mail. Host A is the sending host and host B, receiving.

The following events occur once a mail program has been invoked:

- The User Agent is the component that causes the mail program to begin. It is invoked by a command and it provides an editor for the sender to create a message to be sent.

- After the message is created, it is passed to a Message Transfer Agent. The Message Transfer Agent is responsible for setting up communications with remote hosts and subsequently transmitting the message.

- On the receiving host another Message Transfer Agent accepts the message and stores it on the message queue of the individual receiving the message.

- The recipient of the message views it by invoking the User Agent on his/her machine.

Mail systems are straightforward to use. Besides the SMTP mail system, X.400 is popular. The X.400 mail system is now an ISO standard. It has been, and still is, gaining market share throughout the world. It differs from SMTP in characteristics such as the ability to convert messages to a different medium like faxes, the ability to trace messages via a formal envelope, and a priority system for example.

6.2 Common SMTP Commands

SMTP has a limited number of commands because sending a message is not that complex. Some commands that can be executed against SMTP include:

helo—This command identifies the sender to the receiver.

mail—This invokes SMTP.

send—This causes a message to be delivered directly to the designated recipient if the intended receiver is currently logged on.

soml—This causes message delivery direct to the recipient's display, assuming the recipient is logged on; if not, the message is treated as mail and stored in the recipient's mail box.

help—This asks a recipient for a list of commands supported by the mail system on the host to which he/she is attached.

rcpt—This command can be used to identify an individual recipient. It can be used to identify multiple recipients.

turn—This command is entered by the mail sender to request the recipient to become the sender rather than the receiver.

saml—This command performs two functions. First, it delivers a message to the intended receiver's mail box. And, second, if the intended recipient is logged on, it will deliver the message to the user's display.

Other SMTP commands can be obtained by entering help at the mail prompt.

6.3 Conclusion

SMTP is the electronic mail system specified by RFCs in the TCP/IP protocol suite. Other systems are available and considered public domain (meaning anyone can use them). Electronic mail systems are fairly similar. Most have the ability to send, receive, and store a message. What generally differs with electronic mail is the look and feel.

Chapter 7

TCP/IP Addressing

Examining TCP/IP addressing includes consideration for how applications are addressed. It also involves the IP addressing scheme. If TCP/IP is used with ETHERNET or 802.3 networks, these too need exploration. This chapter looks at all these areas in light of addressing.

7.1 Perspective on Addressing

Before examining specific TCP/IP addressing schemes, consider the correlation of network layers and how they relate to a TCP/IP names and/or address:

Layer	TCP/IP Name(s) and/or Address
User applications	Assigned end user identification
Internet applications	Well-Known-Ports
Transport layer	TCP and/or UDP
Network layer	Internet addresses
LLC sublayer	Local Source Access Point addresses
MAC sublayer	Media Access Control addresses
Physical	Interface Boards

7.2 TCP/IP Port Addressing

TCP/IP applications reside on top of transport protocols, namely TCP and UDP. Each TCP/IP application has an assigned port number. These port numbers are called well-known-ports. These port numbers are published by the Internet Assigned Numbers Authority and are preassigned to identify widely used applications, called well-known-services. For example, TELNET is assigned to TCP port number 23, FTP is assigned to TCP port number 20 and 21 (one is used for FTP data, the other is used for file transfer).

Another example is SMTP; it is assigned to TCP port number 25. Examples of UDP well-known-ports are: Domain Name Server (DNS) residing at port number 53, Simple Network Management Protocol (SNMP) network monitor using port number 161, SNMP traps using port number 162.

Other port numbers exist and are used by TCP and UDP, respectively. Port numbers that are not defined as well-known-ports may be used by custom applications, which is typical of applications using the UDP transport protocol. Port numbers can be changed, and in the UNIX environment, a file called /etc/services is used to administer port numbers.

Ports are end points. They are an addressable entity to create a logical connection. Also known as service contact ports, these ports provide services to callers (requesters) of a particular service. The list below includes the port's decimal number as it is known, the name of the reference associated with a specific port, and a brief description of each port. The list is not exhaustive; it is intended to provide the reader with a reference for common ports used in TCP/IP networks.

Decimal	Name	Description
0		Reserved
1	TCPMUX	TCP Port Service Multiplexer
2-4		Unassigned
5	RJE	Remote Job Entry
7	ECHO	Echo
9	DISCARD	Discard
11	USERS	Active Users
13	DAYTIME	Daytime
15		Unassigned
17	Quote	Quote of the Day
19	CHARGEN	Character Generator
20	FTP-DATA	File Transfer (Data)
21	FTP	File Transfer (Control)

Decimal	Name	Description	(Cont.)
23	TELNET	TELNET	
25	SMTP	Simple Mail Transfer	
27	NSW-FE	NSW User System FE	
29	MSG-ICP	MSG-ICP	
31	MSG-AUTH	MSG Authentication	
33	DSP	Display Support Protocol	
35		Any Private Printer Server	
37	TIME	Time	
39	RLP	Resource Location Protocol	
41	GRAPHICS	Graphics	
42	NAMESERVER	Host Name Server	
43	NICNAME	Who Is	
49	LOGIN	Login Host Protocol	
53	DOMAIN	Domain Name Server	
67	BOOTPS	Bootstrap Protocol Server	
68	BOOTPC	Bootstrap Protocol Client	
69	TFTP	Trivial File Transfer	
79	FINGER	Finger	
101	HOSTNAME	NIC Host Name Server	
102	ISO-TSAP	ISO TSAP	
103	X400	X.400	
104	X400SND	X.400 SND	
105	CSNET-NS	CSNET Mailbox Name Server	
109	POP2	Post Office Protocol version 2	
110	POP3	Post Office Protocol version 3	
111	SUNRPC	SUN RPC Portmap	
137	NETBIOS-NS	NETBIOS Name Service	
138	NETBIOS-DGM	NETBIOS Datagram Service	
139	NETBIOS-SSN	NETBIOS Session Service	
146	ISO-TP0	ISO TP0	
147	ISO-IP	ISO IP	
150	SQL-NET	SQL-NET	
153	SGMP	SGMP	

Decimal	Name	Description	(Cont.)
156	SQLSRV	SQL Service	
160	SGMP-TRAPS	SGMP TRAPS	
161	SNMP	SNMP	
162	SNMPTRAP	SNMPTRAP	
163	CMIP-MANAGE	CMIP/TCP Manager	
164	CMIP-AGENT	CMIP/TCP Agent	
165	XNS-COURIER	Xerox	
179	BGP	Border Gateway Protocol	

7.3 IP Addressing

It is easier to understand TCP/IP addressing by approaching the concept as it relates to a specific host; and this is most true when examining IP addresses. All TCP/IP based hosts use a 32 bit IP address to uniquely identify themselves and the network to which they belong.

This IP address contains three components: the significant bits identifying the address classification, the portion identifying the LAN, and the portion identifying the host. IP address classifications include:

- Class A
- Class B
- Class C
- Class D
- Class E

Class A addresses are typically large networks, class B medium size networks, class C small networks, and class D addresses are used for multicasting, sending a message to a group of hosts connected to the Internet. Class E is virtually unused and considered experimental.

Address classes are important for two reasons. First, if network (X) is connected to the Internet, then (X's) network and host address is assigned by an organization managing Internet. If network (Y) is an organization's or business's internet, the network administrator assigns both network and host addresses.

Address classes provide a way for assigning more networks and fewer hosts, the same amount of networks and the same amount of hosts, and fewer networks and more hosts. Locally administered internets use either class A, B, or C. The addressing scheme uses dotted decimal notation. Knowing the first three digits is enough information to deduce its class. For example, the following first three digits are associated with the class:

- Class A addresses start with a number between 0 - 127.
- Class B addresses start with a number between 128 - 191.
- Class C addresses start with a number between 192 - 223.
- Class D addresses start with a number between 224 - 239.
- Class E addresses start with a number between 240 - 255.

Figure 7.1 illustrates the IP addressing scheme and the correlation of network and hosts addresses.

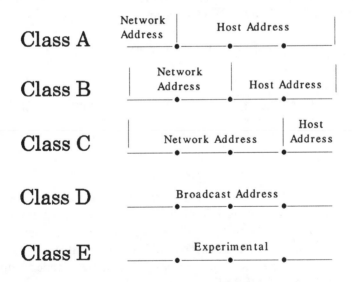

Figure 7.1

An interesting note is that the decimal address 255.255.255.255 is used in some form for masking.

7.4 Sockets

Sockets are the combination of an IP address and the port number appended to it. The socket is that abstract end point used for communication. The socket concept comes from Berkeley based UNIX systems. The socket, in Berkeley UNIX, is an I/O based concept and an end point in the communication process.

7.5 DIX ETHERNET Addressing

If TCP/IP is used with ETHERNET, this form of addressing needs consideration. Digital, Intel, and Xerox (DIX) are behind the ETHERNET specification, and it uses a 48 bit addressing scheme. ETHERNET Network Interface Cards (NICs) come with a preassigned address. However, this can be changed. Each host on an ETHERNET based network must have different ETHERNET addresses. Figure 7.2 shows an example of an ETHERNET frame.

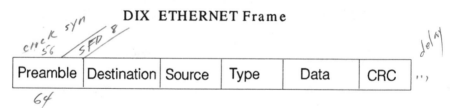

DIX ETHERNET Frame

Preamble	Destination	Source	Type	Data	CRC

Figure 7.2

Before examining the components shown in figure 7.2, additional information needs consideration. Before each ETHERNET frame is sent, the physical layer first transmits a preamble. This preamble is 8 bytes in length and consists of two parts. Technically, it is a sequence of 64 encoded bits providing two pieces of information needed before transmission of the ETHERNET frame.

The first 56 bits of the preamble aid in clock synchronization and to ready both sending and receiving ends prior to transmission. Immediately following these 56 bits are 8 bits known as the start frame delimiter (SFD). The SFD function is to indicate the frame to be transmitted is a valid frame.

At the end of the ETHERNET frame (after the CRC field, which is also known as the Frame Check Sequence FCS) is a transmission delay. This delay functions as a delay sequence providing time for collision detection.

The ETHERNET frame and a brief explanation of its components are:

Component	*Function*
Destination	This field specifies the target for which the frame is intended. This address may be a specific address corresponding to a host, or it can be a multicast address.
Source	This field contains the physical address of the host broadcasting the frame.
Type	This field is not used at the data link layer; instead it is used by higher layers in the network, notably the client layer. It contains a 2 byte value whereby specific vendors determine how it is to be used. In a loose sense this refers to the delivery weight of the frame.
Data	This field is where data resides. The minimum size is 64 bytes, and the maximum size is 1500 bytes.
CRC	This field is where error checking occurs. CRC is the acronym for cyclic redundancy checking. This field has an associated value that is calculated based on the other components of the frame.

In the data field of the ETHERNET frame three pieces of information lead the data field. These are used at the logical link control (LLC) sublayer. They are:

- DSAP—Destination Service Access Point
- SSAP—Source Service Access Point
- Control—Control information used by the LLC sublayer

7.6 802.3 Addressing

Many times an ETHERNET and 802.3 are used synonymously. They are not the same, but they are close. Consider figure 7.3

802.3 Frame

Preamble	Destination	Source	Length	Data	CRC

Figure 7.3

When compared to figure 7.2 (the ETHERNET frame) the obvious difference between an ETHERNET and 802.3 frame is the type and length field in the frame itself. But, differences do not stop here. For example, defined cable characteristics are different. Both version 2.0 and 802.3 define 50 ohm coaxial cable; version 2.0 defines a cable .395 inches in diameter; 802.3 defines a cable diameter of .405 inches. This is enough to cause a conflict, but many vendors circumvent this inconvenience by accommodating both.

Another difference between the two is significant. Transceivers are devices used to connect cables from the interface board to the network backbone. Version 2.0 ETHERNET specifies a Signal Quality Error (SQE) voltage be generated by the transceiver and passed to the interface board to inform the interface board the transceiver is functional. This signal has been dubbed in the marketplace as heartbeat. This is not specified with the 802.3 standard. Hence, a dilemma.

If a version 2.0 ETHERNET interface board is used in conjunction with an 802.3 transceiver, a problem can occur. Since 802.3 transceivers do not necessarily have a heartbeat, if used with a version 2.0 interface, the interface can get confused as to the status of the transceiver. Thankfully, some cooperation in the marketplace happens occasionally! Resolving this has been achieved by vendors manufacturing 802.3 transceivers that are capable of producing heartbeat, thus eliminating the incongruent operation of the two standards. This is generally achieved by changing jumper settings (or with some dip switch settings) to overcome this inconvenience.

7.7 How ETHERNET and 802.3 Emerged

Digital, Intel, and Xerox (DIX) originated ETHERNET version 2.0 standard specifying a type field in the frame. However, this standard (for whatever reason) was not readily acknowledged in national and international communities. In retrospect this was not so much a technical issue as it was a political one (why should we be surprised!).

The IEEE is an organization with a good worldwide reputation. In 1980 the IEEE commissioned a committee named 802 to provide and work with standards for networks, typically LANs. Over time the 802.3 subcommittee had paralleled the ETHERNET version 2.0 standard. This standard differed from the DIX ETHERNET standard because the 802 committee agenda was to conform closely with the International Standards Organization (ISO) to a certain degree.

In short, what developed over a few years was DIX's ETHERNET version 2.0 standard which commanded acceptance in the marketplace. Simultaneously, the 802.3 standard grew in popularity as well. This was fine but differences between the two standards existed; which should not be surprising because two different entities were behind them with different agendas.

The ETHERNET frame had a type field according to the specifications put forth by DIX. On the other hand the 802.3 frame had a length field in the frame. These and other differences existed and still do between the two standards. Ironically, many individuals refer to the two as synonymous, but they are not. What has happened is over time technology has emerged in the marketplace to accommodate both technologies in the same network.

7.8 Conclusion

TCP/IP addressing involves more than just one address. True, normally one address identifies a host—unless that host is multihomed. A multihomed host is known to two or more networks. If this is the case, a host will have two or more distinct internet addresses. An internet address consists of 32 bits. It is typically represented by dotted decimal notation.

Ports are used to identify applications or services that reside on top of TCP or UDP. A list of well-known ports exist that have addresses reflecting particular applications or services.

Sockets are the combination of the internet address and port number. It is an abstract identification of an end point.

ETHERNET uses a 48 bit addressing scheme. This address is also commonly known as a hard address. The ETHERNET address reflects the interface board where the ETHERNET protocol resides.

Often spoken in conjunction with ETHERNET is 802.3. ETHERNET and 802.3 are different. Their differences in the type and length field in the frame is most obvious, but other subtle differences exist. They can work together on the same network, but understanding the differences between the two is required.

Chapter 8

What Is X?

A commonly misunderstood part of TCP/IP is X. Even that statement gets misunderstood. X uses TCP/IP as a network protocol and specifically TCP as a transport protocol, but it does not necessarily have to. However, our focus here will be X in light of TCP/IP. In this chapter enough information is presented so the reader can understand X in relation to other components of TCP/IP. An explanation of what X is, where it came from, its basic components, and how it works is addressed.

8.1 Understanding X

X is not a graphical user interface (GUI), neither is it a window system similar to Microsoft Windows Version 3.1. X is an asynchronous software protocol used to transmit bit-mapped data across a network. It can be implemented with a variety of operating systems and hardware operating platforms. X is not a transport level protocol, but utilizes TCP as a transport mechanism. Figure 8.1 shows the location of X in relation to other parts of network components.

X in relation to other TCP/IP protocols

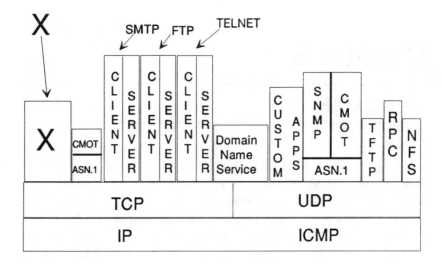

Figure 8.1

X divides application software, also known as clients, like TN3270 emulation applications from display software, known as server software. The former is used for a specific purpose such as logging onto an SNA host and performing data translation on the host where the TN3270 application resides. The software application is the client.

On the other hand, software that *controls* the display is the server. Since display software (known as a server) is separate from application software (known as client software) it can operate locally or on any network host. This works because of the configuration of X software, hosts, and application programs. Collectively, this results in a distributed windowing environment.

The X server program is responsible for two-dimensional drawings on a display. Actually, a server is responsible for everything on the display directly or indirectly. Drawings, however, are the result of "events" generated from a client application, and the server passes messages it receives from a user to the interacting client. Hence, X's event driven architecture.

In short, X provides components that enable a distributed windowing system possible. It is generally called the X window system.

8.2   Origins of X

X is not as old as many think. Its birth can be dated back to the early '80s at MIT's computer science laboratory. It emerged out of a group concentrating on programming languages being developed for distributed computing. This development project involved a number of people working on different programs. Those who have programmed in any language understand that "bugs" (errors in the code) are part of any development project. An individual working on this project focusing on distributed computing concluded that a windowing system would be ideal to expedite working through program bugs. This is part of how the idea behind this windowing system began.

If program bugs were not enough problems, these scientists and researchers were developing programming code for a distributed computing environment (DCE). DCEs were charting new waters at the time, and to complicate matters further they were up against an environment of heterogeneous computers which had fundamental problems with basic communications. Numerous vendors had computers and related devices of all types at MIT. One of the focal points at the time was an intense work group devoted to developing a heterogeneous environment where all computers and devices could communicate with one another in a practically seamless fashion.

Those working on the distributed computing environment project began researching, attempting to determine if anyone (institution, agency, etc.) had explored this concept of a windowing system in a heterogeneous environment before. They discovered work had been done on a windowing system at Stanford. The work at Stanford had been named "W," correlating the abbreviation with windows. For information sake, the associated time frame was approximately 1984.

After working with individuals at Stanford, some at MIT pursued this windows environment and acquired a copy of the "W" software. The copy of windows software from Stanford focused on DEC equipment, but those at MIT were interested in a distributed window environment because of the heterogeneous equipment at MIT. After initial modifications were made to the "W" software from Stanford, MIT's researchers decided to rename it "X."

By 1985, X software had been refined and brought through 6 versions. By mid-1986, X was at version 9. In 1986, SUN MicroSystems announced a product called Network Extended Windowing Systems (NEWS). This announcement added fuel to the fire of X growth because it was so close to X from MIT. In 1987, MIT held an X conference; eleven companies attended and began joint work on X with MIT. The X Consortium (as the eleven companies were dubbed) began taking shape and was formally announced in 1988.

X is now at version 11 release 5. By the end of 1993 X may become X11 R6. Speculation abounds as to the date this release will be stable, but general consensus indicates sometime in spring of 1994.

In short order X took the network (and particularly the LAN) marketplace by storm. It was a perfect (close to perfect) match for the UNIX operating system and the TCP/IP protocol suite. It offered a friendly interface for the UNIX operating system and provided distributed windowing support. Combined with UNIX, TCP/IP, and network growth throughout the 1980s, X seemed to meet a much wanted interface and distributed windowing system. These factors contributed to the proliferation of X.

8.3 X Components

X itself was created with a layered concept; however, the majority of references to X do not explain it this way. X was intended to have maximum portability, and in order to achieve this a layered approach is required. Figure 8.2 depicts X layers, their functions, and associated programs and components.

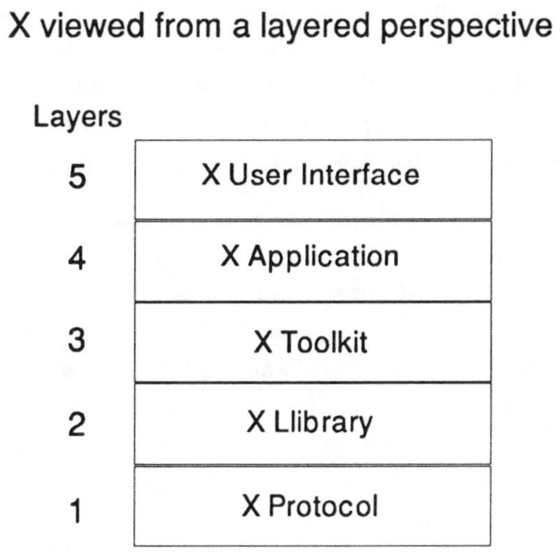

X viewed from a layered perspective

Layers

5	X User Interface
4	X Application
3	X Toolkit
2	X Llibrary
1	X Protocol

Figure 8.2

Examine the following chart with figure 8.2. The chart associates X layers to a function and its associated programs.

Layer	Function	Associated Program/ Function
Layer 5	User Interface	SUN's OPENLOOK OSF's Motif NeXT computer
Layer 4	Application	Window Manager olwm mwm
Layer 3	Toolkit	Xt
Layer 2	X Library	Xlib
Layer 1	X Protocol	components of X software

The topmost layer (what the user interacts with) is the User Interface layer. This layer consists of interfaces such as OPENLOOK from SUN MicroSystems, Motif from the Open Software Foundation (OSF), and NeXT from the NeXT computer corporation, for example. These interfaces prescribe the look and feel of the interface.

Layer 4 is the X application layer. The window manager operates at this layer. As figure 8.2 indicates olwm is the acronym for OPENLOOK Window Manager and mwm is the acronym for Motif Window Manager. A window manager in X actually controls the display. It makes multiple, simultaneous "windows" on one display possible. The window manager provides functions such as being able to resize a "window," invoke pop-up menus, etc. Technically, a window manager itself is a client application running against an X server. Because X was designed for maximum flexibility, it can support different window managers as long as they follow X protocol. Hence, different window managers exist; notably from SUN MicroSystems, OSF, and NeXT.

Layer 3 represents the X toolkit. Multiple toolkits are possible. A toolkit is a collection of high-level programs (routines) created from lower level programming in the Xlibrary. Frequently, toolkits are referred to as Xt. Toolkits provide programmers with specific functions such as menus, scroll bars, etc. Specific routines in a toolkit are commonly referred to as widgets. The benefit of having toolkits is a programmer does not have to start from nothing when creating an X client application.

Layer 2 is the Xlibrary. The Xlibrary is a collection of C language subroutines. The Xlibrary is frequently referred to as Xlib. These routines are the lowest level programming aid in X. Some Xlibrary subroutines provide functions such as drawing, responding to mouse events, and responding to keyboard events to name a few. X version 11 Xlibrary is considered the industry standard and is the base for future enhancements.

Layer 1 is the X protocol. This protocol supports asynchronous, event driven, distributed windowing environments across heterogeneous platforms. When used with TCP/IP X uses TCP as a transport mechanism and resides atop the TCP portion of the transport layer.

8.4 The Function of X

X provides windowing capabilities across heterogeneous operating systems, hardware platforms, network protocols, and network implementations (topologies). It appears different because of the versatility in support built into X for user interfaces and window managers. But, at the lower layers (or closer to the core) of X, you find adherence to X protocol and Xlibrary routines.

Seemingly, X's most prevalent implementation is an interface for the UNIX operating environment. Even though X is not as user friendly as many would like, it is somewhat friendlier than UNIX and other environments it operates within.

8.5 Common Terms Used with X

A point of confusion is terminology used with X. This section includes some basic terms and their definitions. Many other terms are used, but these will orient you to the world of X.

Access Control List—A list of hosts that are allowed access to each server controlling a display is maintained in the /etc/Xn.hosts file. The n here is the number of displays that hosts can access. This list is also called the host access list.

Active Window—This is the window where input is directed.

Background—Windows may have a background that consists of a solid color or a pattern of some kind.

Background Window—The area that covers the entire screen. This is the area that other windows are displayed against. It is also called the root window.

Client—Also known as an X application program. Examples of client programs include terminal emulation programs, window manager programs, and the clock program. Client programs do not have to run on the same program as the display server.

Display—One or more screens driven by an X server. The DISPLAY environment variable dictates to programs which server to connect to unless this is overridden by the -display command line option.

Event—Something that must happen prior to an action occurring in response.

Font—A specific style of text characters.

Font Directory—Referring to the default directory where fonts used with X are stored.

Foreground—This term refers to the pixel value used to draw pictures or text.

Geometry—This is an option that can be used to specify the size and placement of a window on the display screen.

Icon—A symbol representing a window, that when selected by a mouse will cause it to take its original form.

Property—A general term used to refer to the properties of a window. The basic purpose of properties serve as a communication mechanism between clients. For example, windows have properties such as a name, window type, data format, and data within the window.

Server—Software and hardware that provides display services for X clients. The server accepts input from the keyboard and a mouse.

Window—An area on a display created by a client. For example, the xclock.

Window Manager—The window manager is a client program (application). It permits movement, resizing, and other functions to be performed on a display.

8.6 How X Works

Put simply, the X server is responsible for managing a display. Programs that interact with the X server, regardless of their function, are Xclients. Their particular function is program specific. For example, the xclock is considered a client (program) application.

X works differently from MS Windows because it was architecturally designed differently. X was designed to operate in a distributed environment and with multiple hosts, whereas MS Windows was not. From a practical standpoint, this means those pieces that make an X window environment work can reside physically on different machines. Not so with MS Windows; this windowing environment was designed to operate on one machine at a time. Actually, MS Windows is a shell; it is tied to the operating system. Some call MS Windows a graphical user interface (GUI).

Some programs are designed to operate in a windowing environment only. Programs must be designed to operate this way. This is true with X or MS Windows.

In an X environment, code may reside on one physical machine, but not necessarily. With MS Windows, code is physically located on one machine.

Before we explore how X works, some facts need to be presented. For example, the window manager is the major factor in the look and feel of how X works. So if SUN MicroSystems' OPENLOOK window manager is used, then the look and feel of the display will take on its characteristics. On the other hand, if the OSF Motif window manager is used, it will have a different look and feel. The window manager is what a user sees on a display.

The X display server is software that keeps up with input from devices like a keyboard and a mouse. In essence, the display server gets messages from an xclient, then updates the window on the display to reflect that message. Display servers can operate on the same machine as the xclient(s) being used or they may be located on a different machine, or they can even be stored in ROM on special terminals. Hence the term X terminal.

Another aspect about X to remember is that X itself is about graphics. Its purpose is to support graphics in a distributed window environment and by default supports text. For years X has been dominant in environments where UNIX is the operating system and TCP/IP has been the network protocol. X is not confined to UNIX and TCP/IP, but it solves a major problem in UNIX environments for many users; that is, a friendlier user interface. Understanding the interaction of X in such an environment is helpful.

X uses TCP as a transport mechanism. TCP is reliable in the sense it retransmits data if some is lost during transmission. TCP is also connection oriented, maintaining a transport layer protocol connection.

From a user viewpoint X boils down to what is seen on the display. This is deceptive because everything is seen on the display; but if the display is analyzed, we can isolate what is coming from where and how it works! Consider figure 8.3.

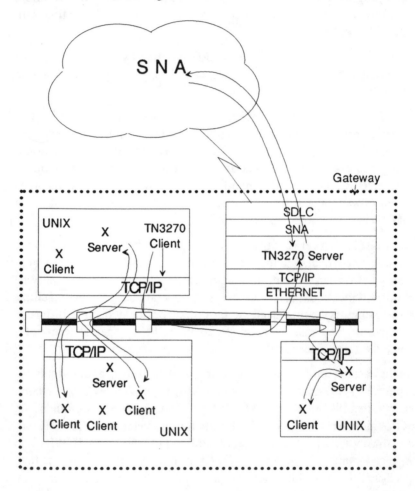

Figure 8.3

Notice what can be deduced from figure 8.3:

- The network is TCP/IP based.
- Three hosts are located on the network.
- Each host is implementing X.
- Each host has an X server.
- Each host has X clients.
- A gateway from the TCP/IP to SNA network is present.
- A TN3270 client program operates under X on one machine.
- The TN3270 client provides required terminal emulation between the TCP/IP network and the SNA network.
- The TN3270 client program communicates with the X server as well as the TN server on the gateway between the two networks. The X part of the TN3270 client program communicates with the X server so the X server can perform the necessary functions for the graphical functions. The TN protocol part of the TN3270 application provides the required terminal emulation between the TCP/IP and SNA networks.
- The TN3270 client program can be executed from any of the hosts on the network. The prerequisite is that a network connection be made between the two hosts first. This means a TELNET or rlogin for example. Once this connection is established, then the TN3270 program can be executed from any host.

In summary, the X environment is complex. It is understandable, but it requires time. I know no shortcuts in this area of technology if your desire is to go beyond just mere button pushing.

8.7 The Environment

The environment must be considered! Part of what makes X complex in the UNIX environment is setting environment variables. This is not overly burdensome, but it does require work. One problem encountered with environment variables is they can be changed on-the-fly thus affecting variables put in place upon logon. Additionally, some Xclient programs have certain variables that must be set in order for the program to work properly.

Common problems with environment variables include: First, setting the appropriate variable in the PATH statement in the .profile can be confusing. Second, because of the complexity of some .profiles they become cumbersome. Third, because of the flexibility of the UNIX, variables can be exported on-the-fly, thus creating additional confusion.

A prudent thing to do if you are working with X and UNIX is spend time with a knowledgeable system administrator who understands both and has the ability to communicate what you need to understand for your particular environment. Based on my mental bruises working with these areas, I suggest this is the best way to begin.

8.8 Conclusion

X provides the means whereby a graphical interface can be achieved. Typical applications used with X are emulators permitting access to SNA environments along with other popular graphical oriented programs. X is not intuitively obvious to learn. It is not like MS Windows, nor was it designed to be. Setup and customization of X and the UNIX operating system requires knowledgeable individuals who understand both environments. Remember, just because a system administrator may understand UNIX does not make him/her an X guru. They are large disciplines to understand. Implemented correctly with adequately trained users, X can report user performance and provide an indication of user satisfaction.

Acronyms

ACB	Access Control Block
ACF	Advanced Communication Function
ACK	Acknowledgement
ANSI	American National Standard Institute
API	Application Programming Interface
APPL	Application
ARP	Address Resolution Protocol
ARPA	Advanced Research Projects Agency
ASCII	American National Standard Code for Information Interchange
ASN.1	Abstract Syntax Notation One
BER	Basic Encoding Rules
BGP	Border Gateway Protocol
BSD	Berkeley Software Distribution
CCITT	International Telegraph and Telephone Consultative Committee
CMIP	Common Management Information Protocol
CMIS	Common Management Information Services
CMOT	Common Management Information Services and Protocol over TCP/IP
CRC	Cyclic Redundancy Check
CSMA/CD	Carrier Sense Multiple Access with Collision Detection
DARPA	Defense Advanced Research Projects Agency
DCE	Distributed Computing Environment
DDN	Defense Data Network
DEC	Digital Equipment Corporation
DEV	Deviation
DFS	Distributed File Service
DISA	Defense Information Systems Agency
DIX	Digital, Intel, and Xerox ETHERNET protocol
DME	Distributed Management Environment
DNS	Domain Name System

DSA	Directory System Agent
DSAP	Destination Service Access Point
DTE	Data Terminal Equipment
DUA	Directory User Agent
EBCDIC	Extended Binary Coded Decimal Interchange Code
EGP	Exterior Gateway Protocol
EOF	End of File
EOR	End of Record
FCS	Frame Check Sequence
FDDI	Fiber Distributed Data Interface
FTAM	File Transfer, Access, and Management
FTP	File Transfer Protocol
FYI	For Your Information
GGP	Gateway to Gateway Protocol
GOSIP	Government Open Systems Interconnection Profile
GTF	Generalized Trace Facility
HDLC	High Level Data Link Control Protocol
IAB	Internet Architecture Board (also known as Internet Activities Board)
IAC	Interpret as Command
IBM	International Business Machines
ICMP	Internet Control Message Protocol
ID	Identifier
IEEE	Institute of Electrical and Electronic Engineers
IESG	Internet Engineering Steering Group
IETF	Internet Engineering Task Force
IGMP	Internet Group Management Protocol
IGP	Interior Gateway Protocol
IP	Internet Protocol
IRTF	Internet Research Task Force
ISDN	Integrated Services Digital Network
ISO	International Standard Organization
ISODE	ISO Development Environment
LAN	Local Area Network
LAPB	Link Access Procedures Balanced

LAPD	Link Access Procedures on the D-channel
LLC	Logical Link Control
MAC	Media Access Control
MAN	Metropolitan Area Network
MIB	Management Information Base
MS	Millisecond
MTA	Message Transfer Agent
MTU	Message Transfer Unit
NETBIOS	Network Basic Input Output System
NFS	Network File System
NIC	Network Interface Card
NREN	National Research and Education Network
NSAP	Network Service Access Point
NSFNET	National Science Foundation Network
NVT	Network Virtual Terminal
OSF	Open Software Foundation
OSI	Open Systems Interconnection
OSPF	Open Shortest Path First
PC	Personal Computer
PDU	Protocol Data Unit
PI	Protocol Interpreter
POP	Post Office Protocol
PPP	Point-to-Point Protocol
RARP	Reverse Address Resolution Protocol
RFC	Request For Comment
RIP	Routing Information Protocol
RMON	Remote Network Monitor
RPC	Remote Procedure Call
RST	Reset
SDLC	Synchronous Data Link Communication
SLIP	Serial Line Interface Protocol
SMTP	Simple Mail Transfer Protocol
SNA	Systems Network Architecture
SNMP	Simple Network Management
SONET	Synchronous Optical Network

SPF	Shortest Path First
SSAP	Source Service Access Point
SSCP	System Services Control Point
SYN	Synchronizing segment
TCB	Transmission Control Block
TCP	Transmission Control Protocol
TELNET	Terminal Networking
TFTP	Trivial File Transfer Protocol
TLI	Transport Layer Interface
TTL	Time-to-Live
UA	User Agent
UDP	User Datagram Protocol
ULP	Upper Layer Protocol
WAN	Wide Area Network
X	X Window System
XNS	Xerox Network Systems

Glossary

Abstract Syntax Notation One (ASN.1)—A language used in OSI and TCP/IP networks to define datatypes for use in network management.

Acknowledgement—A response sent by a receiver to a sender indicating successful reception of data. TCP requires acknowledgements, thus insuring a reliable data transfer mechanism.

Active Open—A client operation performed to establish a TCP connection with a server on a target host.

Address—An identifiable location. A location within memory. A location of a node within a network. A reference to a particular point with a computer or network environment. A way of identifying a network, subnetwork, or node.

Address Mask—A way of omitting certain parts of an IP address in order to reach the target destination without broadcasting an address to unnecessary LAN segments or subnetworks. It is also referred to as a subnet mask. The address mask uses the 32 bit IP addressing scheme, D classification. A variation of 255.255.255.255 is used.

Address Resolution—The mapping of an IP address to a hardware address. In the TCP/IP suite of protocols, Address Resolution Protocol (ARP) performs this function.

Address Space—An identified range of addresses available to an application program.

Agent—An SNMP process, operating in a TCP/IP based host, that responds to both get and set requests; an agent can also send trap messages.

API—Application Program Interface. Defined routines that are callable services by a program.

Application Layer—The topmost player in the OSI reference model that aids in the identification of communicating partners. It performs the following functions: establishes the authority to communicate; supports file services, electronic mail, print services; and transfers information.

ARPA—Advanced Research Project Agency. This is DARPA's former name. ARPA was an agency funded by the government

ARPANET—Advanced Research Projects Agency Network. The packet switching network that became known as the Internet.

ASCII—American National Standard Code for Information Interchange. ASCII is a character set defining alphanumeric characters. Some 128 possible binary arrangements exist.

Assigned Numbers—Request For Comment (RFC) documents that specify values used by the TCP/IP protocol suite.

Asynchronous—Also called async. Without a regular time relationship.

Backbone—A generic term (rather nebulous in its usage) that is used to refer to a set of nodes and links connected together comprising a network. It is also used to refer to the upper layer protocols used in a network. It is used in other ways to refer to the physical media that connects components in a network.

Bandwidth—Refers to the range of frequencies transmitted on a channel. The difference between the highest and lowest frequencies transmitted across a channel.

Baseband—A type of channel where data transmission is carried across only one communications channel. Baseband supports one signal transmission at a time. ETHERNET is an example of baseband technology.

Baseband Signaling—A type of transmission technology used in Local Area Networks. This type transmission is characterized by a continuous encoded signal transmitted over a medium. Only one node at a time may send data over this type transmission technology.

Baud—A unit of measure that reflects the number of times a signal changes state in one second. For example, if a signal only has two states, then the baud rate would be equal to the bit rate (in reference to a binary state).

BER—Bit Error Rate.

Berkeley Software Distribution (BSD)—Typically referred to as Berkeley 4.2 or 4.3, it is UNIX operating system software that includes support for TCP/IP.

BITNET (Because It's Time NETwork)—A network started at the city university of New York. It evolved to connect with over 200 other universities prior to merging with the CSNET producing CREN. It provides electronic mail.

Bit rate—The rate, typically expressed in seconds, that bits are transmitted.

Block Mode—A string of data recorded or transmitted as a unit. Block mode transmission is the normal transmission mode in an SNA environment.

Bridge—A network device capable of connecting networks using similar protocols.

Broadband—A range of frequencies divided into narrow "bands" each of which can be used for different transmission purposes. Also known as wideband.

Broadband signaling—A type of signaling used in Local Area Networks that use analog signals, implement carrier frequencies, and multiplex more than one transmission at a given instance in time.

Broadcast—Simultaneous transmission of the same data to all nodes connected to the network.

Brouter—A network device capable of performing the function of a bridge while simultaneously filtering protocols and/or packets destined for nodes on a different network.

Burst Mode—A transmission mode where data is transmitted in bursts rather than continuous streams.

BSD—Berkeley Software Distribution. This is UNIX based software including support for TCP/IP.

BUS—A linear configuration with respect to network topology.

Cache—An implementation of memory that usually operates faster than core or main memory. It is used to speed data and/or instruction transfer because it is designed to store frequently used data and/or instructions.

Carrier Sense—A signal generated at the physical network layer to inform the data link layer that one or more nodes are transmitting on the underlying medium.

Carrier Sense Multiple Access with Collision Detection (CSMA/CD)—This is a media access control protocol. Nodes using this protocol listen to the medium to which they are attached. As long as there is no signal on the medium being monitored, a node listening can send data across the medium.

Cheapernet—An implementation of ETHERNET where the approximate length of the medium is 200 feet. It utilizes 75 ohm coaxial cable, inexpensive connectors, and requires no transceivers for transmission.

Classification—A means of identifying network types.

Client—A program that can be invoked by a user; a user being a human or a program. Loosely used to refer to a user.

Client/Server Architecture—A general phrase used to refer to a distributed application environment where a program exists that can initiate a session and a program exists to answer the requests of a client. The origin of this concept is most strongly rooted in the TCP/IP protocols.

Client/Server—Terms used to refer to a peer-to-peer method of operation of applications within hosts. Beyond this definition, it is used to convey different thoughts usually defined by a vendor and/or individual making the word nebulous.

CMIP—Common Management Information Protocol. A network management protocol used natively in an ISO environment. When CMIP is used in a TCP/IP environment it is referred to as CMOT.

CMIS—Common Management Information Service. Management related services provided by CMIP.

CMOT—The implementation of CMIP over TCP/IP, where TCP is used as the transport mechanism.

Collision—An event that occurs when two or more nodes broadcast on the same network medium, at the same time.

Collision Detection—The ability of a device to detect if a collision has occurred.

Compile—To translate a program written in a high-level language into machine language. Thus the program is executable.

Connection—A link between two or more entities. Connections may be logical, physical, and/or both.

Connectionless—Referring to a type of network service that does not send acknowledgements upon receipt of data to the originating source.

Connection Oriented—Referring to a type of network service whereby the transport layer protocol sends acknowledgements concerning the condition of the receipt of data from the source host. This type service provides retransmissions if problems have been determined as a result of data transfer.

Contention—A condition in certain LAN implementations where the Media Access Control (MAC) sublayer permits two or more nodes to start transmission while risking collisions.

CREN (Consortium for Research and Education Network)—This is the resulting name from the combination of CSNET and BITNET.

Crosstalk—A term referring to signals that interfered with another signal being transmitted.

CSNET (Computer Science NETwork)—This is a network that offered electronic mail services. It merged with BITNET to form CREN.

Cyclic Redundancy Check (CRC)—A mathematical function used with bits in a frame and included in the frame. It is used for verification purposes in the transmission of frames of data.

Daemon—A program commonly found in different UNIX environments. It operates unattended performing standard services. This type program can be triggered by time intervals for execution.

DARPA—Defense Advanced Research Project Agency.

Data—A generic reference to alphanumeric characters within a computer or related device.

Datagram—A basic unit of data that traverses a TCP/IP internet.

Data Circuit Equipment (DCE)—The required equipment to attach Data Terminal Equipment (DTE) to a line or network for example.

Data Link—The part of a node that is controlled by a data link protocol. It is the logical connection between two nodes.

Data Link Protocol—A prescribed way of handling the establishment, maintenance, and termination of a logical link between nodes. Examples of data link protocols include: Token Ring, ETHERNET, SDLC, etc.

Data Terminal Equipment (DTE)—The source or destination of data. An example would be a terminal attached to a network; in this capacity the terminal would be considered DTE equipment.

DCA (Defense Communication Agency)—This is a governmental agency responsible for the Defense Data Network (DDN) and maintaining lines and other things.

DDN—Defense Data Network. This is a term used loosely to refer to MILNET, ARPANET, and the TCP/IP protocols they employ.

Destination Address—In an ETHERNET network, this refers to the target node address.

Digital—Referring to a state of on or off; representing a binary 1 or a binary 0.

Distributed Computing Environment (DCE)—An Open Software Foundation (OSF) defined set of technologies supporting distributed computing environments.

Directory System Agent (DSA)—A program that interacts with a directory user agent using X.500 protocols. The DSA is a facility that takes queries from Directory User Agents (DUAs). The DSA acquires information from a database to meet the request.

Distributed File Service—An Open Software Foundation (OSF) file server technology.

Directory User Agent—A program that helps a user to send a query to an X.500 directory server. It works in conjunction with DSAs.

Distributed Management Environment (DME)—An Open Software Foundation (OSF) system and network management technology.

Distributed Processing—The act of processing storage; I/O processing, control functions, and actual processing is dispersed among two or more nodes.

Domain Name System—A service used with the TCP/IP protocol suite to replace the previous method of keeping track with host names, aliases, and internet addresses. The domain name service is a distributed database used to convert node names into internet addresses. The concept behind DNS is decentralizing the naming convention through distributing the responsibility for mapping of names and addresses.

Dotted Decimal Notation—A representation of addressing typically used in expressing internet protocol addresses. For example, 137.1.1.100 is an internet address identifying a network and host.

Double Byte Character Set—A character set where alphanumeric characters are represented by two bytes. Examples of languages where this is used include: Japanese, Chinese, and Korean.

Drop Cable—Typically used in an ETHERNET network. It refers to the cable connecting the node to the transceiver attached to the network backbone.

Dumb Terminal—A nonprogrammable terminal.

Dynamic Link Library (DLL)—A programming module that contains dynamic link routines which are linked at load or execution time.

EBCDIC—Extended Binary Coded Decimal Interchange Code. IBM's character set used in SNA. This character set is the foundation where data stream such as 3270, etc. get their components making up a particular data stream.

Emulation—To simulate the real thing.

3270 Emulation—An application program that emulates the functions and 3270 data stream appearing as if it were a genuine 3270 data stream.

Encapsulation—A technique used by layered network protocols where, as data travels down the network layers, headers and trailers are added to represent that layer. For example, when data is passed from an application above the TCP layer, TCP adds a header and trailer, thus encapsulating the data; likewise, this datagram is passed to the IP layer where IP wraps an IP header and trailer around the TCP portion, and so on down the network. When this arrives at the target host, the reverse occurs; that is, as the data travels up the layers, respective headers and trailers are removed.

Enterprise Network—Generally agreed to be a wide area network providing services to all corporate sites. In many instances it has a nebulous meaning, typically defined by the individual or vendor using the term.

ETHERNET—A data link level protocol. It comprises layers one and two when compared to the OSI reference model. It is a broadcast networking technology. ETHERNET can be implemented with different media types, such as thick or thin coaxial cable or copper shielded twisted pair cabling as examples. ETHERNET uses CSMA/CD mechanism to access the medium.

ETHERNET Address—A 48 bit address, commonly referred to as a hard address. This address identifies an ETHERNET network interface card (NIC), thus identifying a host hardware address.

ETHERNET Meltdown—A scenario where the ETHERNET becomes saturated, or nearly to that point. Normally, this phenomenon last only for a short while. It is generally caused by a misrouted or nonvalid packet.

Event—An occurrence. For example, an occurrence significant to a specific task.

FDDI—Fiber Distributed Data Interface. An ANSI defined standard for high speed data transfer over fiber optic cabling.

File Server—A program operating on a host providing access to files from remote hosts.

Fragmentation—The forming of datagrams into pieces. This is required when a datagram is too large to reach its destination.

Frame—Typically, this term refers to data and all TCP/IP headers and trailers including ETHERNET.

Frame Check Sequence (FCS)—A mathematical function used with bits in a frame; and the FCS is appended to the frame. It is used by the receiving end to recalculate the value to determine if an error has occurred.

Frame Relay—A switching mechanism for routing frames as quickly as possible.

FTAM—File Transfer Access Method. This is an OSI file transfer program and protocol. It provides some management functions. It does permit copying files between systems, performing file management functions, and even deleting files.

FTP—File Transfer Protocol. A TCP/IP based application used for transferring (copying) a file (or multiple files) from one system to another. Part of FTP provides password protection.

Full Screen—A term used for how data is displayed on a terminal. As the term connotes, data is displayed one full screen at a time. This is in contrast to line mode where one line of data at a time is displayed.

Gateway—When used with the Internet, traditionally this term referred to a device that performs a routing function. Now the term refers to a networking device that translates all protocols of one type network into all protocols of another type network.

Gigabyte—One billion bytes. When written in decimal notation this means: 1,073,741,824.

GOSIP—Government Open System Interconnection Profile. This is a government standard using the OSI reference model.

Hardware Address—A low-level address associated with each node on the network. This address is generally the address related to the interface card in the node. For example, an ETHERNET address is considered a hard address. In this example, a 48 bit address is used. This address is used by other ETHERNET based hosts to communicate with one another.

Heartbeat—A voltage used with ETHERNET.

High Level Data Link Control (HDLC)—An international data communication standard that specifies a particular order for a series of bits.

Hop count—The number of bridges data crosses in a token ring network.

IAB—Internet Activities Board. A group that coordinates the development of the TCP/IP protocol suite.

ICMP—Internet Control Message Protocol. A protocol that works in conjunction with the Internet Protocol (IP) that handles control and error messages.

IEEE—Institute of Electrical and Electronic Engineers.

IEEE 802.2—A data link standard used with the 802.3, 802.4, and 802.5 standards.

IEEE 802.3—A standard defining the physical layer using CSMA/CD with a BUS topology.

IEEE 802.4—A standard defining the physical layer using token passing with a BUS topology.

IEEE 802.5—A standard defining the physical layer using a token passing technology implemented on a ring topology.

IESG—Internet Engineering Steering Group. This is the executive party of the IETF.

IETF—Internet Engineering Task Force. One group that is part of the IAB; it is responsible for short term engineering needs as they relate to the TCP/IP protocol suite.

Inactive—In SNA, the state of a resource. It means that resource is not operational.

Initiate—To send a request.

Interface—A shared point between two entities, be they software or hardware.

Internet—A collection of networks connected together that span the entire globe. Actually, it is a virtual network. The NFSNET is considered the backbone of the network.

Internet Address—A 32 bit address used to identify hosts and networks.

Interoperability—A case where networks and computer devices of different types are able to communicate effectively.

Interpreter—A program that takes high level language programs and translates them, one line at a time, into machine language. Typically, an interpreter is slower than a compiler because a compiled program is processed prior to execution time, whereas the interpreted program is converted into machine language in real time, immediately before execution.

IP—Internet Protocol. That part of the TCP/IP suite of protocols that handles routing of data.

IP Datagram—This is the basic unit of information passed through a TCP/IP network. This datagram contains source and destination addresses.

IRTF—Internet Research Task Force. A group that is part of the IAB. It concentrates on research and development of the TCP/IP protocol suite.

ISPF—Interactive System Product Facility. An IBM program offering that has full screen editing capabilities.

ISO—International Standard Organization. This is an international standards body which focuses upon deriving standards in various areas.

ISODE—ISO Development Environment. This is a concerted effort to develop software allowing OSI protocols to run on top of TCP/IP.

ISO Reference Model—The networking model created by the International Standard Organization defining seven layers of a network, isolating functions within each layer. It is used as a baseline for comparison/contrast of other network types.

IS-IS—Intermediate System to Intermediate System protocol. It is a routing protocol that performs routing functions with OSI and IP based data.

Jam—A way ETHERNET nodes have of communicating to all nodes on the LAN that a collision has occurred.

Jitter—A scenario that can occur with a 10BaseT network where signals are out of phase with one another.

LAN—Local Area Network. A collection of computer related equipment connected in such a way that communication can occur between all nodes connected to the medium.

Learning Bridge—A special type network device. It serves the function of a bridge, but it has the capability to learn what nodes are connected and route data accordingly.

Leased Line—A dedicated communication line between two points. This type line is a constant vehicle for logical communications to occur at all times. Contrast this with switched line.

Line mode—In regards to displays, this means one line at a time is displayed. Contrast with Full screen.

Link—A generic term used to refer to a connection between two end points.

Logical—A generic term used to refer to convey an abstract meaning or implementation. It is typically the antithesis of Physical.

Logical Link Control (LLC)—The upper part of the data link sublayer protocol responsible for governing the exchange of data between two end points.

MAC—Media Access Control. The lower half of the data link sublayer. It is responsible for framing data and controlling the physical link between two stations.

MAN—Metropolitan Area Network. A network that supports high speeds spanning typically a metropolitan area. The IEEE 802.6 specifies this standard.

Maximum Transmission Unit (MTU)—This is the largest datagram that can traverse a given network such as ETHERNET or Token Ring.

Medium Access Unit (MAU)—A device for central connection of nodes operating in a network.

Menu—A list of choices presented in a preformatted pattern.

MIB—Management Information Base. This is a database containing configuration and statistical information about nodes on a network. It is used in a Simple Network Management Protocol (SNMP) environment. It can maintain information about devices such as hosts, routers, gateways, bridges, brouters, etc.

MILNET (MILitary NETwork)—This network was originally part of the ARPANET. It was sectioned in 1984 for military installations to have reliable network service while research and other aspects of networking were being conducted.

Modem—A device that converts digital signals into analog signals and vice versa.

Modem eliminator—A device that functions as two modems, but in fact is merely providing a service for data terminal equipment (DTE) and data communication equipment (DCE).

Multihomed host—A host attached to two or more networks.

Multiplex—To simultaneously transmit multiple signals over one channel.

MVS—IBM's Multiple Virtual Storage operating system.

Name Resolution—A process of mapping aliases to an address. The domain name system provides a mechanism to perform this function.

National Institute of Standards and Technology (NIST)—A standard body in the United States that promotes communication oriented standards. It used to be called the National Bureau of Standards.

National Research and Education Network (NREN)—A network backbone supporting large capacities planned for use with the Internet in the future.

National Science Foundation Network (NFSNET)—This network is part of the Internet backbone.

NETBIOS—Network Basic Input Output Operating System. An IBM and compatible network programming interface.

Network—A collection of computers and related devices connected in such a way so that effective communication occurs.

Network Address—In TCP/IP networks, this refers to the IP address of a node.

Network File System (NFS)—Sun MicroSystems' protocols that permit clients to mount remote directories onto their own local file system, thus appearing to be local.

Network Interface Card (NIC)—A generic reference for a networking interface board.

Network Information Center (NIC)—A centralized administration facility used with the Internet.

Network Information Service (NIS)—Protocols used to provide a directory service for network information. It was introduced by SUN MicroSystems.

Network Management—Reference to the control mechanism of a network. This may include monitoring, activation, and deactivation.

Network Virtual Terminal (NVT)—A basic set of protocols governing virtual terminal emulation.

Node—A generic term used to refer to varying types of networking devices.

Non-SNA—Meaning not a native SNA device.

Open Shortest Path First (OSPF)—This is an Internet routing protocol that can route data traffic via multiple paths using the knowledge of the Internet's topology to make routing decisions.

Open Software Foundation (OSF)—A group of computer and computer related vendors collaborating to produce technologies for multivendor interoperation.

Open Systems Interconnection (OSI)—A set of ISO standards relating to data communications.

Optical Fiber—Glass or plastic cable used as a communications medium.

Packet—In TCP/IP networks, this refers to that data passing between the internet layer and the data link layer. Technically, a packet includes an IP header, TCP header, and data. The term is also used in a generic sense referring to a defined portion of data transferred throughout the network.

Passive Structure—An action taken on behalf of a TCP/IP server program to prepare it to receive requests from clients.

Pathname—The complete string of information that must be entered into a system in order to access or identify a file.

PING (Packet InterNet Groper)—This is the name of a program used with TCP/IP networks. The program provides a way of testing access to a destination by sending an ICMP echo request, then waiting for a response from the target host.

Point-to-Point—Direct data transmission between two points without intervention from other devices in any way.

Point-to-Point Protocol (PPP)—This protocol has the ability to provide host-to-network and router-to-router connections over synchronous and asynchronous lines.

Port—In TCP/IP, a number used to identify applications. In general, a port is referred to as an entry or exit point. Ports are associated with TCP or UDP transport protocols.

Processor—A central processing unit.

Protocol—A set of rules governing behavior or method of operation.

Protocol Conversion—Changing one type protocol (way of performing a task) to another type protocol.

Protocol Data Unit (PDU)—A generic term used to refer to a unit of data, headers, and trailers at any layer in a network. This term is frequently used in a TCP/IP environment.

Proxy—A mechanism where a system functions for another system when responding to protocol requests.

RARP—See Reverse Address Resolution Protocol.

Remote Network Monitor—A node that collects and maintains information about network traffic.

Remote Procedure Call (RPC)—A specific protocol that permits calling a routine that executes a server; the server returns output and return codes to the caller.

Requests for Comment (RFC)—A set of documents containing TCP/IP protocols. They comprise the TCP/IP protocol suite and are available at the Network Information Center.

Repeater—A network device that repeats signals so the length of a network can be extended.

Resolver—A software program that makes it possible for clients to access the Domain Name System database and acquire an address.

Resource—Generally used to refer to application programs, however it may be used in a general sense to refer to devices such as hardware. A resource can be referred to as being local, remote, network, or other characterizations.

Reverse Address Resolution Protocol (RARP)—A protocol included in the TCP/IP protocol suite that allows a TCP/IP node to acquire its IP address by performing a broadcast on the network.

Retransmission Timeout—A state where a TCP segment of data has been sent to a target node, but an acknowledgement was not received by the sending node in a certain amount of time.

RIP—Routing Information Protocol. A protocol used by the Berkeley BSD UNIX operating systems for exchanging information pertaining to routing. Typically, it is used when a small number of computers are in use.

RISC/6000—IBM's line of processors and workstations that are based on RISC processors. They use the Advanced Interactive Executive (AIX) operating system, which is an implementation of UNIX.

Rlogin—A remote login service provided with the Berkeley BSD UNIX operating system. The service is similar to TELNET application in the TCP/IP protocol suite.

Routine—A program, or part of a program, that serves a specific purpose; normally this purpose is calling another routine to perform a function.

Routing—A process of determining which path is to be used for data transmission.

Routing table—A list of valid paths through which data can be transmitted.

RS-2332-C—A physical layer specification for connecting devices.

SAP—Service Access Point.

Segment—A protocol data unit that consists of TCP header information and optional data. Specifically, it is a unit of data sent from one node's TCP to another node's TCP.

Segment—Parts of a network; typically ETHERNET LANs are divided into parts. These parts are commonly called segments.

Serial—A description of events explaining that the occurrence of events is one after another. Contrast to parallel.

Server—An application that answers requests from clients. The term is dominant in the TCP/IP networking environment. A server can also perform specific functions such as: print, file, terminal, communications, etc. In this sense, a server is used generically.

Simple Mail Transfer Protocol (SMTP)—In TCP/IP, an application including a client and server providing EMAIL services for all hosts with TCP/IP software installed and enabled.

SLIP—Serial Line Internet Protocol. A protocol used to utilize internet protocol over serial lines, such as a switched telephone line.

SNA—Systems Network Architecture. IBM's proprietary networking protocol announced in 1974.

Socket—In TCP/IP, a socket is an addressable point that consists of the IP address and the TCP or UDP port number. Basically, it provides application access to TCP/IP protocols.

Socket Address—The complete designation of a TCP/IP node. It consists of a 32 bit IP address and a 16 bit port number.

Source Routing—A method of delivery (routing) determined by the source node.

Source—The originating entity.

Subnet—In TCP/IP, part of a TCP/IP network identified (isolated) by a portion of the internet address.

Subnet address—In TCP/IP, that part of the IP address that identifies the subnetwork.

Subnet Mask—A way to exclude networks from having a broadcast on certain networks, isolating broadcasts to the desired network(s).

Subroutine—A set of instructions that are executed by a call from another program.

Swapping—A process that moves all program contents from internal to external storage and vice versa.

Switched connection—A data link connection that is similar to a telephone call. The link is established on demand. Thus reference to a switched line. Contrast a leased line.

SYN—This is a segment used in the beginning (start) of a TCP connection. Both source and target hosts exchange the SYN segment with information defining characteristics about the session. It is used to synchronize the target and destination nodes.

Synchronous Data Transfer—The physical transfer of data between two nodes that are clocked, or timed, and a predictable time relationship exists.

TELNET—A TCP/IP application using TCP as a transport mechanism. It consists of a client and server. All TCP/IP protocol suites have this application because it is part of the definition of what makes TCP/IP what it is.

TCP—Transmission Control Protocol. A transport layer protocol that is part of the TCP/IP protocol suite. TCP provides a reliable data stream mechanism performing retransmissions when a positive acknowledgement is not returned to the source from the destination node.

TCP/IP—The acronym for Transmission Control Protocol/Internet Protocol. TCP/IP is an upper layer networking protocol. It is client/server based at the application layer.

10Base2—An uncommon reference to ETHERNET. It literally means 10Megabits per second, using baseband signaling, with a contiguous cable segment length of 100 meters and a maximum of 2 segments.

10Base5—A reference to ETHERNET referring to 10 Megabits per second, using baseband signaling, with 5 continuous segments not exceeding 100 meters per segment.

10Base-T—A general reference to ETHERNET meaning 10 Megabits per second, using baseband signaling and twisted pair cabling.

Telenet—This is a public, packet switched network utilizing X.25 protocol. It is operated by GTE.

Tera—A numeric quantity, when expressed in bytes, one terabyte is denoted as: 1,009,511,627,766.

Terminal Server—A network device that provides physical access for dumb terminals. Most terminal servers have an abbreviated TCP/IP suite of protocols to permit dumb terminal remote logon and other services on the TCP/IP network.

Terminator—A resistor that must be on the ends of a thick and thin-net ETHERNET network. A terminator absorbs spent broadcasts on the network.

TFTP—Trivial File Transfer Protocol. This is a mechanism for remote logons similar to TELNET; but it uses UDP as a transport layer protocol.

Throughput—The amount of data that can be successfully moved across a medium or processed within a certain time period.

Token Ring—A lower layer networking protocol using a token passing method controlling data traffic. It is connection oriented at a data link level.

Topology—The configuration of network devices. Examples include: BUS, Star, Ring, Dual Ring, etc.

Traffic—A generic term used to describe the amount of data on a network backbone at a given period in time.

Transceiver—A network device required in baseband networks. It simply takes a digital signal and puts it on the analog baseband medium. Transceivers are devices that sense collisions.

Transmission Class 4 (OSI TP4)—This is an OSI transport layer protocol similar to TCP in the TCP/IP protocol suite.

UDP—User Datagram Protocol. A transport layer protocol in the TCP/IP protocol suite. It does not perform retransmissions. Contrast to TCP.

User Agent—This is an electronic mail program that helps end users to manage messages, both incoming and outgoing.

User Service—Service provided by TCP permitting an application to specify that data being transmitted is urgent and should be processed as soon as possible.

Virtual—Appearing to exist, but in reality the appearance is achieved by functions or processes.

Well Known Port—In TCP/IP, an address for an expressed purpose generally agreed upon by TCP/IP users.

Wide Area Network (WAN)—The term usually refers to a network spanning large geographic distances.

Workstation—This term connotes different meanings to different individuals. For example, it could be used to refer to a PC, an RISC based processor, or even a dumb terminal. At best its meaning is arbitrary.

X.400—A protocol defining standards for electronic mail in an open network.

X.500—A protocol defining standards for directory services in an open network.

X Series—A collection of standards widely accepted; included are data communication protocols.

XNS—Xerox Networking Standard. The Xerox corporation network protocols. These protocols are similar to TCP/IP, but they are different.

X Window—A software protocol developed at MIT for a distributed windowing system. It uses TCP for a transport protocol and provides flexibility so users on multiple hosts can benefit from a distributed windowing system.

Appendix A
Well-Known-Port Numbers

TCP and UDP transport mechanism use Well Known Ports. These port names reflect specific applications of wide implementation and usage. Ports are the end points; an addressable entity to create a logical connection. Also known as service contact ports, these ports provide services to callers (requesters) of a particular service. The following list includes the port's decimal number as it is known, the name of the reference associated with a specific port, and a brief description of what each port provides. The list is not exhaustive; it is intended to provide the reader with a reference for common ports used in TCP/IP networks.

Decimal	Name	Description
0		Reserved
1	TCPMUX	TCP Port Service Multiplexer
2-4		Unassigned
5	RJE	Remote Job Entry
7	ECHO	Echo
9	DISCARD	Discard
11	USERS	Active Users
13	DAYTIME	Daytime
15		Unassigned
17	Quote	Quote of the Day
19	CHARGEN	Character Generator
20	FTP-DATA	File Transfer (Data)
21	FTP	File Transfer (Control)
23	TELNET	TELNET

Decimal	Name	Description	(Cont.)
25	SMTP	Simple Mail Transfer	
27	NSW-FE	NSW User System FE	
29	MSG-ICP	MSG-ICP	
31	MSG-AUTH	MSG Authentication	
33	DSP	Display Support Protocol	
35		Any Private Printer Server	
37	TIME	Time	
39	RLP	Resource Location Protocol	
41	GRAPHICS	Graphics	
42	NAMESERVER	Host Name Server	
43	NICNAME	Who Is	
49	LOGIN	Login Host Protocol	
53	DOMAIN	Domain Name Server	
67	BOOTPS	Bootstrap Protocol Server	
68	BOOTPC	Bootstrap Protocol Client	
69	TFTP	Trivial File Transfer	
79	FINGER	Finger	
101	HOSTNAME	NIC Host Name Server	
102	ISO-TSAP	ISO TSAP	
103	X400	X.400	
104	X400SND	X.400 SND	
105	CSNET-NS	CSNET Mailbox Name Server	
109	POP2	Post Office Protocol version 2	
110	POP3	Post Office Protocol version 3	
111	SUNRPC	SUN RPC Portmap	
137	NETBIOS-NS	NETBIOS Name Service	
138	NETBIOS-DGM	NETBIOS Datagram Service	
139	NETBIOS-SSN	NETBIOS Session Service	
146	ISO-TP0	ISO TP0	
147	ISO-IP	ISO IP	
150	SQL-NET	SQL-NET	
153	SGMP	SGMP	
156	SQLSRV	SQL Service	

Decimal	Name	Description	*(Cont.)*
160	SGMP-TRAPS	SGMP TRAPS	
161	SNMP	SNMP	
162	SNMPTRAP	SNMPTRAP	
163	CMIP-MANAGE	CMIP/TCP Manager	
164	CMIP-AGENT	CMIP/TCP Agent	
165	XNS-COURIER	Xerox	
179	BGP	Border Gateway Protocol	

Appendix B
RFC Listing

This appendix contains Request For Comment (RFC) numbers and their association. The date related to this RFC is also included. This section sheds a bit of history about the development of the parts of TCP/IP and OSI as well. Other topics are also covered in these RFCs.

The list is not exhaustive. But it provides enough information to point you in the right direction.

PARAMETERS, REQUIREMENTS, AND USEFUL INFORMATION

rfc1340	Assigned numbers. 1992 July
rfc1250	IAB official protocol standards. 1991 August
rfc1208	Glossary of networking terms. 1991 March
rfc1180	TCP/IP tutorial. 1991 January
rfc1178	Choosing a name for your computer. 1990 August
rfc1175	FYI on where to start: A bibliography of internetworking information. 1990 August
rfc1173	Responsibilities of host and network managers: A summary of the "oral tradition" of the Internet. 1990 August
rfc1166	Internet numbers. 1990 July

rfc1127	Perspective on the Host Requirements RFCs. 1989 October
rfc1123	Requirements for Internet hosts—application and support. 1989 October
rfc1122	Requirements for Internet hosts—communication layers. 1989 October
rfc1118	Hitchhikers guide to the Internet. 1989 September
rfc1011	Official Internet protocols. 1987 May
rfc1009	Requirements for Internet gateways. 1987 June
rfc980	Protocol document order information. 1986 March

LOWER LAYERS

rfc1236	IP to X.121 address mapping for DDN IP to X 121 address mapping for DDN. 1991 June
rfc1220	Point-to-Point Protocol extensions for bridging. 1991 April
rfc1209	Transmission of IP datagrams over the SMDS Service. 1991 March
rfc1201	Transmitting IP traffic over ARCNET networks. 1991 February
rfc1188	Proposed standard for the transmission of IP datagrams over FDDI networks. 1990 October
rfc1172	Point-to-Point Protocol (PPP) initial configuration options. 1990 July
rfc1171	Point-to-Point Protocol for the transmission of multiprotocol datagrams over Point-to-Point links. 1990 July
rfc1149	Standard for the transmission of IP datagrams on avian carriers. 1990 April

rfc1055	Nonstandard for transmission of IP datagrams over serial lines: SLIP. 1988 June
rfc1044	Internet Protocol on Network System's HYPERchannel; Protocol specification. 1988 February
rfc1042	Standard for the transmission of IP datagrams over IEEE 802 networks. 1988 February
rfc1027	Using ARP to implement transparent subnet gateways. 1987 October
rfc903	Reverse Address Resolution Protocol. 1984 June
rfc895	Standard for the transmission of IP datagrams over experimental Ethernet networks. 1984 April
rfc894	Standard for the transmission of IP datagrams over Ethernet networks. 1984 April
rfc893	Trailer encapsulations. 1984 April
rfc877	Standard for the transmission of IP datagrams over public data networks. 1983 September

BOOTSTRAPPING

rfc1084	BOOTP vendor information extensions. 1988 December
rfc951	Bootstrap Protocol. 1985 September
rfc906	Bootstrap loading using TFTP. 1984 June

IP AND ICMP

| rfc1219 | On the assignment of subnet numbers. 1991 April |
| rfc1112 | Host extensions for IP multicasting. 1989 August |

rfc1088	Standard for the transmission of IP datagrams over NetBIOS networks. 1989 February
rfc950	Internet standard subnetting procedure. 1985 August
rfc932	Subnetwork addressing scheme. 1985 January
rfc922	Broadcasting Internet datagrams in the presence of subnets. 1984 October
rfc919	Broadcasting Internet datagrams. 1984 October
rfc886	Proposed standard for message header munging. 1983 December
rfc815	IP datagram reassembly algorithms. 1982 July
rfc814	Name, addresses, ports, and routes. 1992 July
rfc792	Internet Control Message Protocol. 1981 September
rfc791	Internet Protocol. 1981 September
rfc781	Specification of the Internet Protocol (IP) timestamp option. 1981 May

ROUTING PROTOCOLS

rfc1267	A Border Gateway Protocol 3 (BGP-3). 1991 October
rfc1247	OSPF version 2. 1991 July
rfc1222	Advancing the NSFNET routing architecture. 1991 May
rfc1195	Use of OSI IS-IS for routing in TCP/IP and dual environments. 1990 December
rfc1164	Application of the Border Gateway Protocol in the Internet. 1990 June
rfc1163	Border Gateway Protocol (BGP). 1990 June
rfc1074	NSFNET backbone SPF based Interior Gateway Protocol. 1988 October

rfc1058	Routing Information Protocol. 1988 June
rfc904	Exterior Gateway Protocol formal specification. 1984 April
rfc827	Exterior Gateway Protocol (EGP). 1982 October
rfc823	DARPA Internet gateway. 1982 September
rfc1136	Administrative Domains and Routing Domains: A model for routing in the Internet. 1989 December
rfc911	EGP Gateway under Berkeley UNIX 4.2. 1984 August 22
rfc888	"STUB Exterior Gateway Protocol." 1984 January

ROUTING PERFORMANCE AND POLICY

rfc1254	Gateway congestion control survey. 1991 August
rfc1246	Experience with the OSPF protocol. 1991 July
rfc1245	OSPF protocol analysis. 1991 July
rfc1125	Policy requirements for inter-Administrative Domain routing. 1989 November
rfc1124	Policy issues in interconnecting networks. 1989 September
rfc1104	Models of policy based routing. 1989 June
rfc1102	Policy routing in Internet protocols. 1989 May

TCP/UDP

rfc1072	TCP extensions for long-delay paths. 1988 October
rfc896	Congestion control in IP/TCP internetworks. 1984 January

rfc879	TCP maximum segment size and related topics. 1983 November
rfc813	Window and acknowledgement strategy in TCP. 1982 July
rfc793	Transmission Control Protocol. 1981 September
rfc768	User Datagram Protocol. 1980 August

FILE TRANSFER/ACCESS

rfc1094	NFS: Network File System Protocol specification. 1989 March
rfc1068	Background File Transfer Program (BFTP). 1988 August
rfc959	File Transfer Protocol. 1985 October
rfc949	FTP unique named store command. 1985 July
rfc783	TFTP Protocol (revision 2). 1981 June
rfc775	Directory oriented FTP commands. 1980 December

TERMINAL ACCESS

rfc1205	Telnet 5250 interface. 1991 February
rfc1198	FYI on the X window system. 1991 January
rfc1184	Telnet Linemode option. 1990 October
rfc1091	Telnet terminal type option. 1989 February
rfc1080	Telnet remote flow control option. 1988 November
rfc1079	Telnet terminal speed option. 1988 December
rfc1073	Telnet window size option. 1988 October
rfc1053	Telnet X.3 PAD option. 1988 April

rfc1043	Telnet Data Entry Terminal option: DODIIS implementation. 1988 February
rfc1041	Telnet 3270 option. 1988 January
rfc1013	X Window System Protocol, version 11: Alpha update. 1987 June
rfc946	Telnet terminal location number option. 1985 May
rfc933	Output marking Telnet option. 1985 January
rfc885	Telnet end of record option. 1983 December
rfc861	Telnet extended options: List option. 1983 May
rfc860	Telnet timing mark option. 1983 May
rfc859	Telnet status option. 1983 May
rfc858	Telnet Suppress Go Ahead option. 1983 May
rfc857	Telnet echo option. 1983 May
rfc856	Telnet binary transmission. 1983 May
rfc855	Telnet option specifications. 1983 May
rfc854	Telnet Protocol specification. 1983 May
rfc779	Telnet send location option. 1981 April
rfc749	Telnet SUPDUP Output option. 1978 September
rfc736	Telnet SUPDUP option. 1977 October
rfc732	Telnet Data Entry Terminal option. 1977 September
rfc727	Telnet logout option. 1977 April
rfc726	Remote Controlled Transmission and echoing Telnet option. 1977 March
rfc698	Telnet extended ASCII option. 1975 July

MAIL

rfc1341	MIME (Multipurpose Internet Mail Extensions) Mechanisms for Specifying and Describing the Format of Internet Message Bodies. 1992 June
rfc1143	Q method of implementing Telnet option negotiation. 1990 February
rfc1090	SMTP on X.25. 1989 February
rfc1056	PCMAIL: A distributed mail system for personal computer. 1988 June
rfc974	Mail routing and the domain system. 1986 January
rfc822	Standard for the format of ARPA Internet Text messages. 1982 August
rfc821	Simple Mail Transfer Protocol. 1982 August

DOMAIN NAME SYSTEM

rfc1035	Domain names—implementation and specification. 1987 November
rfc1034	Domain names—concepts and facilities. 1987 November
rfc1033	Domain administrators operations guide. 1987 November
rfc1032	Domain administrators guide. 1987 November
rfc1101	DNS encoding of network names and other types. 1989 April
rfc974	Mail routing and the domain system. 1986 January
rfc920	Domain requirements. 1984 October
rfc799	Internet name domains. 1981 September

OTHER APPLICATIONS

rfc1196	Finger User Information Protocol. 1990 December
rfc1179	Line printer daemon protocol. 1990 August
rfc1129	Internet time synchronization: The Network Time Protocol. 1989 October
rfc1119	Network Time Protocol (version 2) specification and implementation. 1989 September
rfc1057	RPC: Remote Procedure Call Protocol specification: Version 2. 1988 July
rfc1014	XDR: External Data Representation standard. 1987 June
rfc954	NICNAME/WHOIS. 1985 October
rfc868	Time Protocol. 1983 May
rfc867	Daytime Protocol. 1983 May
rfc866	Active users. 1983 May
rfc865	Quote of the Day Protocol. 1983 May
rfc864	Character Generator Protocol. 1983 May
rfc863	Discard Protocol. 1983 May
rfc862	Echo Protocol. 1983 May

NETWORK MANAGEMENT

rfc1271	Remote network monitoring Management Information Base. 1991 November
rfc1253	OSPF version 2: Management Information Base. 1991 August
rfc1243	AppleTalk Management Information Base. 1991 July
rfc1239	Reassignment of experimental MIBs to standard MIBs. 1991 June

rfc1238	CLNS MIB for use with Connectionless Network Protocol (ISO 8473) and End System to Intermediate System (ISO 9542). 1991 June
rfc1233	Definitions of managed objects for the DS3 Interface type. 1991 May
rfc1232	Definitions of managed objects for the DS1 Interface type. 1991 May
rfc1231	IEEE 802.5 Token Ring MIB. 1991 May
rfc1230	IEEE 802.4 Token Bus MIB. 1991 May
rfc1229	Extensions to the generic interface MIB. 1991 May
rfc1228	SNMP-DPI: Simple Network Management Protocol Distributed Program Interface. 1991 May
rfc1227	SNMP MUX protocol and MIB. 1991 May
rfc1224	Techniques for managing asynchronously generated alerts. 1991 May
rfc1215	Convention for defining traps for use with the SNMP. 1991 March
rfc1214	OSI internet management: Management Information Base. 1991 April
rfc1213	Management Information Base for network management of TCP/IP-based internets: MIB-II. 1991 March
rfc1212	Concise MIB definitions. 1991 March
rfc1187	Bulk table retrieval with the SNMP. 1990 October
rfc1157	Simple Network Management Protocol (SNMP). 1990 May
rfc1156	Management Information Base for network management of TCP/IP-based internets. 1990 May

rfc1155   Structure and identification of management information for TCP/IP-based internets. 1990 May

rfc1147   FYI on a network management tool catalog: Tools for monitoring and debugging TCP/IP internets and interconnected devices. 1990 May

rfc1089   SNMP over Ethernet. 1989 February

SECURITY

rfc1244   Site Security Handbook.

rfc1115   Privacy enhancement for Internet electronic mail: Part III 1989 August

rfc1114   Privacy enhancement for Internet electronic mail: Part II 1989 August

rfc1113   Privacy enhancement for Internet electronic mail: Part I 1989 August

rfc1108   Security Options for the Internet Protocol. 1991 November

TUNNELING

rfc1241   Scheme for an internet encapsulation protocol: Version 1.

rfc1234   Tunneling IPX traffic through IP networks. 1991 June

rfc1088   Standard for the transmission of IP datagrams over NetBIOS networks. 1989 February

rfc1002   Protocol standard for a NetBIOS service on a TCP/UDP transport. 1987 March

rfc1001   Protocol standard for a NetBIOS service on a TCP/UDP transport. 1987 March

OSI

rfc1240	OSI connectionless transport services on top of UDP: Version 1. 1991 June
rfc1237	Guidelines for OSI NSAP allocation in the Internet. 1991 July
rfc1169	Explaining the role of GOSIP. 1990 August
rfc1148	Mapping between X.400(1988) / ISO 10021 and RFC 822. 1990 March
rfc1142	OSI IS-IS Intra-domain Routing Protocol. 1990 February
rfc1086	ISO-TPO bridge between TCP and X.25. 1988 December
rfc1085	ISO presentation services on top of TCP/IP networks. 1988 December
rfc1070	Use of the Internet as a subnetwork for experimentation with the OSI network layer. 1989 February
rfc1069	Guidelines for the use of Internet-IP addresses in the ISO Connectionless-Mode Network Protocol. 1989 February
rfc1008	Implementation guide for the ISO Transport Protocol. 1987 June
rfc1006	ISO transport services on top of the TCP: Version 3. 1987 May
rfc995	ISO End System to Intermediate System Routing Exchange Protocol for use in conjunction with ISO 8473. 1986 April
rfc994	ISO Final text of DIS 8473, Protocol for Providing the Connectionless-mode Network Service. 1986 March
rfc982	Guidelines for the specification of the structure of the Domain Specific Part (DSP) of the ISO standard NSAP address. 1986 April

rfc941   International Organization for Standardization. ISO Addendum to the network service definition covering network layer addressing. 1985 April

rfc905   ISO Transport Protocol specification ISO DP 8073. 1984 April

MISCELLANEOUS

rfc1251   Who's who in the Internet: Biographies of IAB, IESG, and IRSG members. 1991 August

rfc1207   FYI on Questions and Answers: Answers to commonly asked "experienced Internet user" questions. 1991 February

rfc1206   FYI on Questions and Answers: Answers to commonly asked "new Internet user" questions. 1991 February

Index